Essential Readings ON Fluency

Compiled and introduced by Timothy V. Rasinski

INTERNATIONAL
Reading Association
800 BARKSDALE ROAD, PO BOX 8139
NEWARK, DE 19714-8139, USA
www.reading.org

The International Reading Association attempts, through its publications, to provide a forum for a wide spectrum of opinions on reading. This policy permits divergent viewpoints without implying the endorsement of the Association.

Executive Editor, Books   Corinne M. Mooney
Developmental Editor   Charlene M. Nichols
Developmental Editor   Tori Mello Bachman
Developmental Editor   Stacey L. Reid
Editorial Production Manager   Shannon T. Fortner
Design and Composition Manager   Anette Schuetz

Project Editor   Rebecca A. Stewart

Cover   design by Linda Steere

The publisher would appreciate notification where errors occur so that they may be corrected in subsequent printings and/or editions.

Library of Congress Cataloging-in-Publication Data

Essential readings on fluency / Timothy V. Rasinski, editor.
    p. cm.
ISBN 978-0-87207-808-6
1. Oral reading. 2. Reading--Remedial teaching. I. Rasinski, Timothy V.
LB1573.5.E87 2009
372.45'2--dc22

2009021963

Contents

About the Editor

Timothy V. Rasinski is a professor of literacy education at Kent State University. He has written more than 200 articles and has authored, coauthored, or edited more than 50 books or curriculum programs on reading education. He is author of a best-selling book on reading fluency entitled *The Fluent Reader*, published by Scholastic, and coauthor of the award-winning fluency program called *Fluency First*, published by the Wright Group. His scholarly interests include reading fluency and word study, reading in the elementary and middle grades, and readers who struggle. His research on reading has been cited by the National Reading Panel and has been published in journals such as *Reading Research Quarterly*, *The Reading Teacher*, *Reading Psychology*, and the *Journal of Educational Research*. Tim is currently writing the fluency chapter for Volume 4 of the *Handbook of Reading Research*.

Tim recently served a three-year term on the Board of Directors of the International Reading Association and from 1992 to 1999 he was coeditor of *The Reading Teacher*, the world's most widely read journal of literacy education. He has also served as coeditor of the *Journal of Literacy Research*. Rasinski is past president of the College Reading Association, and he has won the A.B. Herr and Laureate Awards from that organization for his scholarly contributions to literacy education.

Prior to coming to Kent State, Tim taught literacy education at the University of Georgia. He also worked for several years as an elementary and middle school classroom and Title I teacher in Nebraska. He may be reached by e-mail at trasinsk@kent.edu.

Introduction

Fluency: The Essential Link From Phonics to Comprehension

Timothy V. Rasinski

Prior to the release of the report of the National Reading Panel (National Institute of Child Health and Human Development [NICHD], 2000), reading fluency was a relatively unknown concept in reading education. Many reading teachers were not familiar with reading fluency: it generally was not a significant part of reading teacher training programs, nor did it figure prominently in textbooks on reading education. However, in its review of research related to effective reading instruction, the National Reading Panel (NRP) provided convincing evidence that if you are interested in growing readers, reading fluency is an instructional priority you must address.

My own journey into reading fluency began in the late 1970s and early 1980s, when I was a reading intervention teacher and graduate student in reading education. I was working with some elementary students that I had trouble figuring out. These were clearly bright students who seemed able to decode words they encountered in their reading and who understood the words they read. When I read to them they had a solid understanding of those passages. And yet—despite their intelligence, despite their strengths in word decoding and vocabulary, despite their ability to comprehend texts read to them—when they were asked to read on their own, their comprehension faltered. How could it be that such bright students experienced difficulty in reading?

In my graduate work my professional reading led me to some studies and papers that were beginning to revisit the concept of fluency as it applied to the reading program. Papers by Jay Samuels, Carol Chomsky, Richard Allington, Peter Schreiber, Paul Hollingsworth, and other literacy and language scholars were showing me that there was a critical and often ignored link between reading words and reading comprehension—and that link was reading fluency. I got on that reading fluency horse about 30 years ago, and I have been on it ever since. And although fluency may not be the answer to every student's problems in reading, reading comprehension, and overall reading achievement, it is the answer, or at least part of the answer, to many reading problems. I am convinced that for reading instruction at all levels to be most effective, reading fluency must be a substantial and integral part of the curriculum.

With this compendium of professional resources, I hope that I might lead you down that same professional growth path that I took many years ago. Since my initial forays in this area, much has been written about reading fluency in our professional journals and books. I hope to guide you in a professional development journey through some of the same articles that shaped my own thinking about the nature of fluency and how it is best taught and monitored. I have selected some of the best materials from the professional archives of the International Reading Association to include in this book, and, in the reference list to this introduction, you will find other outstanding resources that I also recommend. I hope you enjoy the journey. Let's begin.

Essential Readings on Fluency, edited by Timothy V. Rasinski. © 2009 by the International Reading Association

Defining Reading Fluency

Perhaps the best place to initiate an exploration of reading fluency is by defining the concept. The multidimensional nature of reading fluency has led to its having different definitions. And each definition of reading fluency leads to different instructional applications for students and teachers.

Let's start by invoking Noam Chomsky's (1964) notion of the different levels or structures of language. The surface structure refers to the observable part of language: in speech, this would be the sounds of language that are produced when we talk with one another; in reading or written language, the surface level refers not only to the sounds made when reading orally, but also to the internal language sounds that we hear when we read silently, and the print that represents those sounds. The deep structure refers to the meaning that is conveyed through speech in oral language and through the printed word in reading. In reading we call the deep structure comprehension.

Clearly, comprehension is the essential goal of reading (or speech). Fluency, however, deals with those surface-level aspects of reading and written language—the print and the sounds represented by the print. Although fluency may not be comprehension, I think of it as the gateway to comprehension. Readers need to have control of the surface-level aspects of written language in order to comprehend what they read. Many students (including my own students described earlier in this introduction) have difficulty understanding what they read, not because they don't have the ability to make meaning, but because they have difficulty breaking through the surface structure of the text. They have trouble decoding words, knowing what the words mean, reading the words automatically, and reading the words with appropriate and meaningful expression.

So, what do readers have to do to break through the surface level of texts? First they need to read words accurately and know what the words mean. Instruction in these areas is part of the word-study component of the reading curriculum. I like to think of word study (including phonics, spelling, and vocabulary) as the groundwork or base for fluency.

However, accuracy with words is not enough. Students need to develop fluency over the surface level of texts. First, readers need to be automatic in their processing of the surface features of the text. That is, they need to be able to decode and understand the written words they encounter in text so automatically or effortlessly that they can direct their limited amount of cognitive energy or attention to the more important task in reading—comprehension.

When readers are not automatic in their surface processing they tend to use too much of their cognitive resources for word recognition. Even if they may read the words correctly and know what the words mean, there is a price to be paid. By using their resources for the lower level task of word recognition, readers have fewer resources available for making meaning. And, as a result, their comprehension falters.

Automaticity was first described in a theoretical paper by LaBerge and Samuels (1974). Once readers develop automaticity in their word recognition, they can move on to higher level tasks such as grouping words into meaningful phrases, accessing their background knowledge related to the topic of the text, making predictions about the passage, making connections to other readings or concepts, developing mental images related to the passage, as well as other strategies and activities that are related to comprehension.

How does one achieve automaticity in the surface-level processing of text? The answer, of course, is practice. In the same way that musicians and athletes rehearse or practice in order to develop effortless control over basic processes, readers need to practice reading in order to develop automaticity. One analogy that is often used to describe automaticity is that of driving a car. Although driving is largely an automatic task for most of us, it required much more attention and concentration when we were first learning to drive. Perhaps you remember having to turn off the radio and refrain from conversing with a passenger when you were learning to drive. Initially, driving required total concentration. However, with much practice over the years, we became automatic in our driving. Proof of our automaticity comes when we drive and now find that we can, at the same time, listen to the radio, CD, or iPod, or converse with a passenger. We are so automatic we can now engage in more than one task at the same time. And, in reading, that other task readers can now engage in is making meaning from the written words.

The first article I have selected to include in this book, Richard Allington's classic "Fluency: The Neglected Reading Goal," was one of the first pieces of professional literature that helped me conceptualize reading fluency, especially as it applied to reading development. Allington argued that one goal of reading fluency instruction should be to help readers develop automaticity in their word recognition. And, he said, that is done through practice.

Allington also pointed to another dimension of fluency, one that links fluency to the actual making of meaning while reading. Prosody or expressiveness in oral language (including oral reading) helps convey meaning. It is not just words that express meaning, but the way those words are expressed and interpreted orally. When we think of someone who is a fluent speaker or reader, we often immediately think of someone who uses his or her voice to add to the meaning of the words. They phrase the text into syntactically appropriate chunks or phrases, they emphasize words, they use dramatic pauses, they raise and lower their voice, they speed up, and they slow down. All these prosodic features allow the language user to make and convey meaning that goes beyond the written word alone.

Allington cited the work of linguist Peter Schreiber in suggesting that prosody is a part of fluency that needs to be considered and addressed in reading instruction. Schreiber (1980) noted that words can be interpreted or understood differently by the way they are phrased. Take, for example, this sentence:

Woman without her man is nothing!

Read one way, the sentence suggests that a female cannot do much without a male. Read or phrased another way, and the meaning of the sentence reverses itself completely. Schreiber noted that appropriate phrasing of written texts is essential to understanding and that phrase boundaries are not always marked by written punctuation. So how do readers know how to phrase text if phrases are not marked for them? Schreiber pointed out that in oral language, phrase boundaries are marked by prosodic cues—pausing and lengthening of the final sound within a phrase. He suggested that readers have to apply their knowledge of prosody in oral language and apply it to written language in order to phrase and understand text appropriately.

Thus, Schreiber and Allington suggest that prosody as well as automaticity need to be part of fluency instruction in order for students to make the full link from word accuracy to comprehension. And, by the way, how do Schreiber and Allington suggest that prosody be developed in reading instruction? In the same way that automaticity is developed: practice!

And so, we now view fluency as a two-dimensional concept including automaticity and prosody or expression. We also place reading fluency between word accuracy and comprehension. Once students are accurate in their word recognition they need to develop automaticity over words. Thus, word recognition is linked to fluency. Once they are automatic in their word recognition, they need to use their cognitive resources to make meaning, and one way to make or embellish meaning is to use one's prosodic voice. Thus, when readers read with expression, even when that expression is internal, they are linking fluency to comprehension.

Teaching Fluency

Because fluency has been shown, theoretically and empirically, to be related to reading comprehension and achievement, it only makes sense to assume that instruction in fluency should lead to improvements in reading comprehension and achievement. Several reviews of research into fluency have concluded that fluency is related to comprehension (Chard, Vauhgn, & Tyler, 2002; Kuhn & Stahl, 2003; NICHD, 2000; Rasinski & Hoffman, 2003). Moreover, these studies identified several effective methods for teaching fluency. In an article I wrote more than 20 years ago, "Fluency for Everyone: Incorporating Fluency Instruction in the Classroom," I outlined the key methods for teaching fluency in classrooms and clinical settings.

Modeling Fluent Reading

Before students can become fluent readers they need to have an understanding of what fluent reading is. Too many students today define fluency as nothing more than reading fast. This is the unintended consequence of having students practice reading primarily to increase their reading rate. As "Fluency for Everyone" describes, an appropriate antidote to the message of fast reading to students is to model fluent reading for students. When teachers or others read to students they have the opportunity to provide a model of what fluent reading should be. In their review of research on fluency strategies for students identified as learning disabled, Chard et al. (2002) recommend modeling fluent reading as a productive strategy for improving reading fluency and overall reading achievement.

When reading to students teachers need to be sure to read with meaningful and appropriate expression or prosody. Moreover, teachers should talk with students about how their oral fluency helped add to the meaning of the passage. Comments like "Did you notice how I read faster in this section and slower in this section? How did that help you understand the meaning of the passage?" can help students understand that they need to attempt to read with similar levels of prosody themselves. At times teachers can read in a distinctively disfluent voice so that students realize that less than fluent reading can detract from a reader's comprehension of a text. Reading to students regularly has the potential for improving motivation for reading, building reading vocabulary, and aiding reading comprehension. Reading to students also has the potential for helping students develop an internal understanding of what is meant by fluency in reading.

Repeated Readings

Earlier in this introduction I noted that reading practice was central to developing both automaticity and prosody. In most instructional settings wide reading is the type of practice that most students engage in. Indeed, wide reading is the most common form of reading in and out of school. In wide reading a reader will read a passage (story, article, book, report, etc.), respond to it in some way, and then move on to another reading.

For some readers, beginning and struggling readers in particular, wide reading may not be enough to ensure adequate progress in reading. Some students read a text once, and they don't read it very well. Rather than move on to the next piece, they may get more benefit out of practicing the original piece or a portion of the original piece several times until they can read it well. We call this type of practice repeated readings.

S. Jay Samuels introduced us to repeated readings in his classic article entitled "The Method of Repeated Readings" that initially appeared in *The Reading Teacher* (*RT*) in 1979. (It was subsequently reprinted in 1997 in the 50th anniversary volume year of that journal.) Samuels had struggling learners read short passages several times until they achieved a predetermined level of fluency. Once achieved, students moved on to a new passage that was as challenging or more challenging than the first. Samuels found that as students practiced a piece they improved on the piece they practiced. More important, however, when they moved on to a new passage, students' initial reading of the new piece was better than their initial reading of the previous passage. This improvement from one passage to the next is evidence of growth or learning transfer as a result of repeated reading.

Subsequent to Samuels's initial research, many studies have demonstrated the power of repeated readings in improving reading performance (e.g., Dowhower, 1987; Herman, 1985). In the 1986 article "Paired Repeated Reading: A Classroom Strategy for Developing Fluent Reading," Pat Koskinen and Irene Blum describe an interesting adaptation of repeated readings. Repeated readings done on one's own can become a bit tedious. Koskinen and Blum suggest that having students work with a partner—one student reading a passage several times while the partner listens, follows along silently, and reacts to the reading—can make repeated readings more engaging for students as they help one another move toward fluency.

Assisted Reading

Complementing repeated reading in fluency instruction is assisted reading. Assisted reading is a form of reading in which a reader reads a text while simultaneously hearing it read to him or her in a fluent manner. For younger or struggling readers, listening to a fluently read passage while reading it at the same time can be quite helpful in facilitating their own fluency development. An early approach to assisted reading called the neurological impress method was described by Heckelman (1969). In impress reading a tutor and student sit next to each other and read aloud the same text simultaneously. The student also points to the text while reading. The tutor directs his or her voice into the ear of the student. In his study Heckelman reported remarkable results from using the impress method in brief tutoring sessions with struggling readers.

Elements of the neurological impress approach were later adapted by psychologist Keith Topping. In his article "Paired Reading: A Powerful Technique for Parent Use," Topping describes how assisted reading can be used by parents and children at home. (See also Topping, 1989.) Rather than direct one's voice into the ear of the reader, in paired reading the student and parent (or other adult) sit side by side and read aloud the same text simultaneously. The student points to the text to ensure that he or she is visually tracking the text while reading. Topping reported that students who did paired reading with their parents on a daily basis made 3 to 5 times the growth in various dimensions of reading achievement, including comprehension, than they had previously experienced. "The Akron Paired Reading Project," an article I wrote with Anthony Fredericks, describes a successful implementation of paired reading in a school setting with struggling readers.

Although we may normally think of assisted reading as occurring when a more advanced reader reads with a less advanced reader, it can take other forms as well. Technology provides us with the ability to record a proficient reading of a text that can be played and replayed for multiple students who read the same text. Again the research behind this form of assisted reading is clear and convincing. Paul Hollingsworth described such an approach in his article entitled "An Experimental Approach to the Impress Method of Teaching Reading." (See also Hollingsworth, 1970.) Students read passages while simultaneously listening to the same passages that had been previously recorded using the technology of the day. Working with struggling readers in the upper elementary grades, Hollingsworth found that 62 fifteen-minute sessions of this form of assisted reading over the course of one semester led to a year's growth in reading.

Carol Chomsky (1976) reported similarly that simply teaching students to decode words was not enough to ensure progress in reading. She described an approach to fluency instruction that involved having students read texts while listening to prerecorded versions of the same texts read with appropriate automaticity and prosody. As with Hollingsworth, Chomsky reported that this form of assisted reading resulted in growth in reading among students who had previously been making minimal growth.

In "Teaching Reading With Talking Books," another article from the 1970s, Marie Carbo reported that having students work with recorded audiobooks can have a profound impact on their development as readers. With this approach (also discussed in Carbo, 1981), students hear a fluent rendering of the text while reading on their own. Of course, this begs the question, Where can teachers come up with such materials for assisted reading? Certainly there are wonderful commercial materials available (e.g., at Carbo's own website, www.nrsi.com). Another approach, interestingly enough, I believe comes from teachers and students themselves. Can you imagine yourself recording books and other texts for your students? Can you imagine your students creating recordings of favorite passages for younger students? Can you imagine your own students wanting to go to the listening center to read and listen to recorded passages made by their friends? Can you imagine those students practicing the passages in order to read with automaticity and meaningful expression for their friends? The possibility of having some students practice and record passages (repeated readings) for other students to read while listening (assisted reading) creates a win–win situation for all students and a way to make fluency instruction using authentic literature for real purposes an integral part of classroom life. Carbo does caution that when teachers or students do make recorded books for their classrooms, they need to be sensitive to reading at the appropriate rate and with appropriate expression so that a struggling reader who is reading and listening will be able to follow along with ease.

Performance Reading

Modeled, repeated, and assisted reading have been well documented as effective approaches for improving reading fluency, and in doing so, improving overall reading achievement. Despite the robust findings that support these approaches, teachers are often faced with the question of how to integrate repeated and assisted reading into their classroom literacy curricula. Asking students to read a text three, four, or five times after having it read to them for the primary purpose of increasing reading rate does not seem to be an authentic literacy activity. Readers do not normally read a text over and over for no meaningful reason.

When looking for an authentic and engaging reason to read a text more than once I found myself thinking of the notion of reading performance. Actors will practice or rehearse lines of a script repeatedly without objection when they know they will be performing that passage to an audience at some time in the future. Thus, the next question we need to ask in our study of reading fluency is this: Will practice done in anticipation of a reading performance lead to gains in reading fluency and overall reading achievement? This is a legitimate question, for as

teachers we should always try to make the types of instructional activities we use with students as authentic as possible. The types of reading we do in the classroom should reflect the kinds of reading that are done outside of the classroom. I am a great advocate of authentic oral reading performance such as that seen with Readers Theatre. The term Readers Theatre appears with different spelling and punctuation in different sources. The International Reading Association has adopted this form in its current style guide, but many authors and experts use a different style.

One of the first studies to explore the use of authentic repeated readings in a classroom and their impact on students' achievement was published in 1998. In "'I Never Thought I Could Be a Star': A Readers Theatre Ticket to Fluency" by Miriam Martinez, Nancy L. Roser, and Susan Strecker, second grade teachers attempted to see if having students repeatedly read and then perform scripts would affect reading achievement. After an implementation of only a few months, students engaged in Readers Theatre made remarkable progress, experiencing more than a year's growth in overall reading and about twice the growth seen among students not involved in the performances. In this article you will note that students doing Readers Theatre also made twice the gain in reading rate over students who did not participate in the performances. These gains in rate (or, more precisely, automaticity) came without any urging or emphasis on speed of reading. Indeed, in Readers Theatre the repeated readings done in rehearsals are aimed at conveying meaning through one's voice, not at reading fast.

Over the years I have had the opportunity to work with some excellent teachers. A few years ago I teamed up with Lorraine Griffith, a fourth-grade teacher in Buncombe County, North Carolina. I had made a presentation in her school district on reading fluency and had talked about performance; she decided to give it a go. She focused on having students practice a poem, script, or other text throughout the week and then take part on Friday in a Readers Theatre festival, poetry slam, or other form of performance. Within months of beginning her program Lorraine was writing to me about the remarkable gains made by her students through this approach to fluency. After several years of finding great growth through her fluency focus, we decided that teachers throughout the country would like to learn about the approach she developed to teaching fluency authentically and engagingly in her classroom. Our article "A Focus on Fluency: How One Teacher Incorporated Fluency With Her Reading Curriculum" was published in October 2004 in *RT*. In this article we report three years of data from Lorraine's class. Her students made on average 2.9 years' worth of growth in reading achievement in the one year they were in her class. Average gains in reading rate more than doubled the increases we would normally expect among fourth graders. Moreover, Lorraine's students found great joy in their reading instruction and made remarkable gains in their own belief in themselves as readers.

In "'I Thought About It All Night': Readers Theatre for Reading Fluency and Motivation," Jo Worthy and Kathryn Prater show that they are also strong advocates of making oral reading performance an integral part of classroom reading instruction. In their article, they provide an excellence rationale for the use of Readers Theatre and great practical suggestions for making it work in the classroom.

Poetry also lends itself well to oral performance for an audience. In a 2008 article in *RT*, "Building Fluency, Word-Recognition Ability, and Confidence in Struggling Readers: The Poetry Academy," Lori Wilfong tells her own story of making poetry the vehicle for student repeated reading (rehearsal) and performance. She provides details of how she developed a Poetry Academy in an elementary school in her community. Students engaged in her weekly poetry practice and performance routine made gains in word recognition, fluency, comprehension, and self-confidence that were well above what would normally have been expected.

We know from the research studies that repeated and assisted reading do work to improve student fluency and overall reading proficiency. The studies shared in this section extend the research to show that repeated and assisted reading

do not have to be done in an instructional environment that provides the message that fluency is all about practicing passages in order to read them as fast as possible. Fluency instruction can be developed in ways that are authentic. Students practice texts that are meant to be read orally for real purposes such as performance. And when they do this, they gain as readers—not only in fluency, but also in overall reading achievement, in increased reading pleasure, and in self-confidence as readers.

Silent Reading Fluency

Reading fluency is normally viewed as an oral reading activity. The articles that I have discussed up to this point deal most prominently with oral reading. However, if reading fluency is to have any instructional value it needs to demonstrate improvements in students' silent reading performance as well as their oral reading. Silent reading is the most ubiquitous form of reading, so any effective reading instructional method needs to have a positive impact on silent reading performance.

Oral repeated and assisted readings have been shown to lead to improvements in students' overall silent reading performance. Such findings suggest that oral reading fluency is internalized into silent reading and expressed as improvements in silent reading performance. This then begs the question, Is it possible to improve silent reading fluency directly and thus improve silent reading proficiency? This may be a more efficient way to teach fluency, or at the very least could be added to the instructional methods available for teaching fluency.

The NRP, however, has suggested that there is no evidence to suggest that practice in silent reading improves fluency or general reading proficiency (NICHD, 2000). Hence, we now have situations in schools where sustained silent reading or other forms of independent silent reading are discouraged.

It seems reasonable to infer that any form of reading, oral or silent, should lead to improvements in reading. The key is to ensure that students are actually reading and that they are reading material that is appropriate for their instructional reading levels. In "Scaffolded Silent Reading: A Complement to Guided Repeated Oral Reading That Works!" Ray Reutzel, Cindy Jones, Parker Fawson, and John Smith tested this hypothesis. In this approach, readers are made accountable for the reading they do, the materials they read are at an appropriate level, and the teacher has an opportunity to interact with students about their reading. Reutzel and colleagues report significant gains in reading fluency and comprehension that are commensurate with gains found in forms of oral reading. This study suggests that oral and silent reading play complementary roles in developing students' fluency and overall reading achievement. Informed teachers now have another tool for moving students toward more fluent reading and add variety into the reading curriculum at the same time.

Measuring Fluency

Tools for measuring students' levels of achievement and growth are essential in education. Without such tools we would not be able to determine growth or identify those students who are not achieving up to expected levels. Because fluency is made up of two key components, automaticity and prosody, measurement tools are required for each of those components.

Automaticity is most commonly measured by reading rate, which is determined by the number of words read correctly from a grade-level passage in a 60-second period (Deno, 1985; Rasinski, 2004). The speed with which a student processes a text provides an indication of their automaticity in word recognition. And, because automaticity is a prerequisite for reading comprehension, reading rate is strongly correlated with measures of reading comprehension and overall reading (Rasinski, 2004). Reading rates that are within appropriate norms provide evidence that students are more automatic and efficient in recognizing words and thus are able to attend more to meaning. Rates that are below norms suggest that the reader is less automatic in word recognition, must attend more to decoding words, and

has less attention available for making meaning. Thus, comprehension suffers.

Through extensive testing of children, Jan Hasbrouck and Gerry Tindal have developed reading rate norms for students in grades one through eight for various times of the school year. These are presented in their 2006 article, "Oral Reading Fluency Norms: A Valuable Assessment Tool for Reading Teachers."

Reading rate is quick and simple to measure. It can be measured in discrete units (words correct per minute), and students normally make substantial and measurable gains in reading rate over the course of a school year. For these reasons, it is a popular measurement tool. But because of its correlation with comprehension, schools are using it more and more to measure progress not only in reading automaticity, but also in overall reading achievement. This reliance on reading rate as a measure of general reading progress has led to some unintended consequences. Reading rate, not automaticity, has become the instructional goal for fluency in many classrooms around the United States. School administrators at the national, state, and local levels are mandating that teachers teach reading rate; teachers are encouraging students to read faster; and many students are beginning to think that proficient reading is nothing more than reading fast. On more than one occasion, students in our own reading clinic here at Kent State University, when presented with a passage from the informal reading inventory, have asked the clinician if they should read the passage as fast as possible.

It is important for students to read with some degree of efficiency and rate, as I describe in my article "Speed Does Matter in Reading." However, the current overarching emphasis on rate is having a negative effect on reading. Jay Samuels (2007) has expressed his concerns about how this approach to the measurement of fluency has lead to a change in the way fluency is conceptualized and taught—as I do as well in the last article included in this collection, "Reading Fluency Instruction: Moving Beyond Accuracy, Automaticity, and Prosody." I recommend that when reading rate is assessed students should be prompted in advance that their best and most expressive reading is desired, not their fastest reading. Moreover, Samuels has noted that because fluency and comprehension are integrally related, fluency should never be assessed without ensuring that students are simultaneously prompted to read for comprehension.

To measure fluency comprehensively we also have to examine the prosodic side of students' oral reading. For classroom purposes, prosody is best measured by a trained teacher listening to a student read and rating the expressive or prosodic quality of the reading on some guiding rubric. Research sponsored by the United States Department of Education found a strong relationship between teacher assessments of oral reading prosody on a rubric and silent reading comprehension (Daane, Campbell, Grigg, Goodman, & Oranje, 2005; Pinnell et al., 1995). Students whose oral reading prosody was rated high had the highest scores on tests of silent reading comprehension. Every drop in oral reading prosody was marked by corresponding drops in silent reading comprehension. In a recent study, Rasinski, Rikli, and Johnston (in press) found similar relationships between oral reading prosody and silent reading comprehension for third-, fifth-, and eighth-grade students. These relationships suggest that prosody is indeed related to overall reading proficiency and that it is well worth measuring in students.

In the article that opens this collection, Dick Allington provides a simple rubric that is easy and quick to use. Other rubrics for prosodic reading can be found in my own volumes on reading fluency (Rasinski, 2003) and reading fluency assessment (Rasinski, 2004).

With these tools for measuring both automaticity and prosody, teachers now have the ability to screen students for fluency difficulties, to assess students regularly to ensure that adequate progress is being made, and to provide intervention for those students who are observed not to be making adequate progress.

Conclusions

I hope you have enjoyed sharing my journey in reading fluency. More important, I hope that this journey has helped you understand the importance of reading fluency and its appropriate place in literacy instruction for all students. Let me end our journey by sharing with you what I think are the important concepts about fluency that I have learned through the years.

First, reading fluency is important in children's literacy development and it is worth teaching. To become a good reader means developing some degree of fluency over or ease in processing the written word. Many students have difficulty in understanding what they read, not because of a difficulty in understanding language, but because of a difficulty in breaking through the written code—processing texts accurately, automatically, and with meaningful expression.

Second, reading fluency is *not* reading fast or making students read fast. Reading rate may be an indicator of reading fluency. However, making students read faster will not achieve the goal of fluency in reading. Automaticity, a component of reading fluency, may be measured by reading rate. However, reading rate is not the same as fluency or automaticity. Rate may be an indicator of automaticity; however, rate in reading is not automaticity and it is not achieved by trying to read ever faster. Gains in automaticity in word recognition are best achieved through wide and deep reading.

Third, the most important ways to teach fluency are through modeling fluent reading for students, guided repeated reading, and assisted reading (or reading while listening to a fluent reading of the same text). Finding ways to make modeling, repeated, and assisted reading authentic and engaging experiences for students is where the art of teaching reading (Rasinski, 2007) meets the science of teaching reading. Teachers who are able to make fluency instruction more than learning to read fast help students understand that reading fluency aids comprehension. Like all reading instruction, fluency should ultimately be about making meaning from the printed word. One way to do this is to make reading an authentic performance activity where students practice reading to perform for an audience. This leads us to the consideration of scripts, dialogues, monologues, poetry, songs, speeches, and other texts meant to be aloud to a listening audience as the appropriate texts for reading fluency instruction.

Fourth, keep in mind that the ultimate goal of reading instruction is to improve silent reading comprehension. Although fluency is generally thought of as an oral reading activity, the ultimate goal is improvement in silent reading performance. If we can find ways to make fluency instruction include silent reading we are likely to find a shortcut to fluency improvements.

Fluency in reading is not the goal of reading instruction. Comprehension, particularly in silent reading, is the goal. However, fluency is a necessary part of reading comprehension, oral and silent. Focusing on fluency is an appropriate and necessary goal of reading instruction, but only to the extent to which it improves the ability of readers to make meaning from what they read. In all your work in fluency, keep that in mind. Fluency needs to lead to and be part of comprehension. Without a focus on meaning while reading, fluency is an empty shell.

References

Carbo, M. (1981). Making books talk to children. *The Reading Teacher, 35*(2), 186–189.

Chard, D., Vaughn, S., & Tyler, B. (2002). A synthesis of research on effective interventions for building reading fluency with elementary students with learning disabilities. *Journal of Learning Disabilities, 35*(5), 386–406.

Chomsky, C. (1976). After decoding: What? *Language Arts, 53*(3), 288–296.

Chomsky, N. (1965). *Aspects of the theory of syntax.* Cambridge, MA: MIT Press.

Daane, M.C., Campbell, J.R., Grigg, W.S., Goodman, M.J., & Oranje, A. (2005). *Fourth-Grade Students Reading Aloud: NAEP 2002 Special Study of Oral Reading.* Washington, DC: U.S. Department of Education, Institute of Education Sciences.

Deno, S.L. (1985). Curriculum-based measurement: The emerging alternative. *Exceptional Children, 52*(3), 219–232.

Dowhower, S.L. (1987). Effects of repeated reading on second-grade transitional readers' fluency and comprehension. *Reading Research Quarterly, 22*(4), 389–407.

Heckelman, R.G. (1969). A neurological impress method of remedial-reading instruction. *Academic Therapy Quarterly, 4*(4), 277–282.

Herman, P.A. (1985). The effect of repeated readings on reading rate, speech pauses, and word recognition accuracy. *Reading Research Quarterly, 20*(5), 553–564.

Hollingsworth, P.M. (1970). An experiment with the impress method of teaching reading. *The Reading Teacher, 24*(2), 112–114, 187.

Kuhn, M.R., & Stahl, S.A. (2003). Fluency: A review of developmental and remedial practices. *Journal of Educational Psychology, 95*(1), 3–21.

LaBerge, D., & Samuels, S.J. (1974). Toward a theory of automatic information processing in reading. *Cognitive Psychology, 6*, 293–323.

National Institute of Child Health and Human Development. (2000). *Report of the National Reading Panel: Teaching children to read: An evidence-based assessment of the scientific research literature on reading and its implications for reading instruction. Reports of the subgroups.* (NIH Publication No. 00-4754). Washington, DC: U.S. Government Printing Office.

Pinnell, G.S., Pikulski, J.J., Wixson, K.K., Campbell, J.R., Gough, P.B., & Beatty, A.S. (1995). *Listening to children read aloud: Data from NAEP's integrated reading performance record at grade 4.* Washington, DC: U.S. Department of Education, Office of Educational Research and Improvement.

Rasinski, T.V. (2003). *The fluent reader: Oral reading strategies for building word recognition, fluency, and comprehension.* New York: Scholastic.

Rasinski, T.V. (2004). *Assessing reading fluency.* Honolulu, HI: Pacific Resources for Education and Learning. Available at www.prel.org/products/re_/assessing-fluency.htm

Rasinski, T.V. (2007). Teaching reading fluency artfully. In R. Fink and S.J. Samuels (Eds.), *Inspiring reading success: Interest and motivation in an age of high-stakes testing* (pp. 117–140). Newark, DE: International Reading Association.

Rasinski, T.V., & Hoffman, J.V. (2003). Oral reading in the school literacy curriculum. *Reading Research Quarterly, 38*(4), 510–522.

Rasinski, T.V., Rikli, A., & Johnston, S. (in press). Reading fluency: More than automaticity? More than a concern for the primary grades? *Literacy Research and Instruction.*

Samuels, S.J. (2007). The DIBELS tests: Is speed of barking at print what we mean by reading fluency? *Reading Research Quarterly, 42*(4), 563–566.

Schreiber, P.A. (1980). On the acquisition of reading fluency. *Journal of Reading Behavior, 12*(3), 177–186.

Topping, K. (1989). Peer tutoring and paired reading. Combining two powerful techniques. *The Reading Teacher, 42*(7), 488–494.

Fluency: The Neglected Reading Goal

Richard L. Allington

A lack of fluency in oral reading is often noted as a characteristic of poor readers, but it is seldom treated. Oral fluency rarely appears as an instructional objective in reading skills hierarchies, teacher's manuals, daily lesson plans, individualized educational plans, or remedial intervention. However, the lack of fluency of most poor readers, usually described as word-by-word reading, is noted in 10 recently reviewed textbooks on reading difficulties, in teacher's descriptions of poor readers' behaviors, in most commercial diagnostic tests of reading ability, and in research describing poor readers (e.g., Clay & Imlach, 1971; Collins, 1982; Resnick, 1970).

Several authors have suggested methods for improving fluency (Allington, 1977; Aulls, 1982; Chomsky, 1978; Cunningham, 1979; Samuels, 1979; Smith, 1979). Others have provided empirical evidence that fluency is trainable and that fluency training improves overall reading ability (Chomsky, 1978; Dahl & Samuels, 1974; Martin & Meltzer, 1976, 1978; Morgan & Lyon, 1979; Neville, 1968). Other authors simply argue the need for fluency (Clay, 1979).

From various sources, then, we see that oral fluency is regarded as a necessary feature in defining good reading. Support also exists for providing training to develop fluency, at least during the reading acquisition phase, and several methods with an empirical base are available for the purpose.

Why hasn't oral reading fluency become a major focus of beginning reading or early remedial instruction? This article explains that a lack of fluency is mistakenly viewed as simply symptomatic of poor reading, suggesting that the poor reader is inefficient in word recognition or analysis.

Typical is Samuels's argument that the nonfluent reader is "nonautomatic in decoding," resulting in reading that is "slow and halting, without expression." This interpretation, commonly accepted by teachers, unfortunately often leads to further instruction in letters, sounds, or words in isolation, in the mistaken belief that more attention to this area will result in improved reading.

A Surprising Study

This assumption was the basis for the Dahl and Samuels (1974) study of a high-speed word recognition program compared with two other instructional treatments. The surprising finding was that "repeated readings," which focused on developing oral reading speed and fluency, produced better achievement than did the program that developed automatic word recognition.

While Samuels (1979) attempted to explain these results in a manner congruent with automaticity theory (LaBerge & Samuels, 1974), Schreiber (1980) pointed out that the explanation inadequately addressed the issue of just which skills produced the achievement gain. Merely learning to recognize words quickly did not produce fluent reading. On the other hand, lack of training in rapid word recognition did not hinder the repeated readings group. So what did the repeated readings group learn?

Schreiber (1980) suggested that the students learned how to put words together in meaningful phrases even though a written text provides few phrasing cues. He noted that written English

Reprinted from Allington, R.L. (1983). Fluency: The neglected reading goal. *The Reading Teacher, 36*(5), 556–561.

uses few graphic signals for prosodic features of the language. In oral language, phrase boundaries are generally marked through pitch, stress, and juncture.

In addition, Schreiber reported evidence that children rely heavily on such prosodic features in understanding speech, more so than do adults. The lack of prosodic markings in written language, then, presents a potential problem for children, some of whom develop adequate word recognition and word analysis skills—they can pronounce accurately every word—without learning to group these words into phrases, particularly on an initial reading.

In learning to understand speech, children rely heavily on the prosodic features that mark meaningful units, and, in fact, they learn to produce some prosodic features of language before learning to produce words (deVilliers & deVilliers, 1978). Infants use intonation to signal query, labeling, surprise, anger, and other expressions before they produce clearly articulated and well-formed sentences. As Schreiber (1980) notes, if children consistently use prosodic features to understand language aurally, they may have difficulty moving beyond accurate word recognition to fluent oral reading given the absence of "signals in the written version that correspond to prosodic cues."

How Children Learn to Phrase

If this transition is difficult, what explains the fact that second graders can parse written sentences into phrases, even though they receive little explicit instruction in such behavior? At this point, no straightforward answer is available, but let's consider several reasonable hypotheses as to why most beginning readers do move from a word level of reading to the phrase level, but also why some do not.

Hypothesis 1. Children with a varied background of reading experiences understand that fluent reading, or prosodic reading, is the goal. We know that children who have been read to (by parents primarily) have a distinct advantage when learning to read (Durkin, 1974–1975). Perhaps the modeling of fluent oral reading

teaches children to use the unmarked prosodic features. "Memory reading" and "invented reading" (Amarel, Bussis, & Chittenden, 1977) are the best exemplars of the influence of modeling. Prereaders who have memorized a favorite story do not recite it word for word; rather, they give a fluent oral rendition. Similarly, with invented reading children produce a story line in response to illustrations in a new book.

In any event, we have a rich tradition supporting reading to children and even a limited empirical base for teacher modeling as a means of improving oral reading fluency in disabled readers (Smith, 1979).

Hypothesis 2. Successful beginning readers receive more encouragement to "read with expression." Too often, slow first grade learners receive large doses of letter, sound, and word instruction, to the neglect of larger units of text-like sentences and stories. To develop "automaticity" in the poorer readers, teachers tend to focus their instruction on the smallest textual units (Gambrell, Wilson, & Gantt, 1981) and they direct attention to these text features when poorer students are reading (Allington, 1980b). Good readers are more likely to get "meaning-oriented" instruction (Alpert, 1974; Gambrell, Wilson, & Gantt, 1981) and to have their attention focused on "making sense" or "sounding right" when reading orally (Allington, 1980a).

Collins (1982) notes several differences in the prosody of good and poor first grade readers and argues that these differences stem from instructional behaviors. Early on, teachers consistently emphasized decoding and accuracy with the less successful group, orienting them toward somewhat staccato oral reading. This emphasis was less prominent in lessons of good readers and they progressed from word reading to phrase reading due to the instructional emphasis provided by their teachers.

Hypothesis 3. Fast learners are given greater opportunities for reading, so they moved more rapidly through the transition to fluency. Large differences in the amount of contextual reading assigned to high and low reader groups have been documented (Allington, 1980a, 1982). Perhaps these greater amounts facilitate acquisition of the ability to parse sentences into phrases and to read orally with appropriate prosody. Samuels (1979) argues that since amount of practice in athletics and music correlates with improvement in performance, practice in reading should lead to better reading performance.

Hypothesis 4. Successful readers are more often reading material that is relatively easy for them, thereby facilitating the transition to fluent reading. Several investigators have reported that poorer readers are more often working with material that is difficult for them (Gambrell, Wilson, & Gantt, 1981; Jorgenson, 1977; Rubin, 1975; Weinstein, 1976). This may inhibit their development of fluent oral reading, since Cecconi, Hood, and Tucker (1977) have demonstrated that passage difficulty exerts a negative impact on oral prosody. In this latter study, average readers' oral fluency was inhibited when passages were above their achievement levels. Regular and sustained exposure to difficult reading material may limit children's apprehension of appropriate grammatical junctures and other prosodic cues.

Hypothesis 5. Silent reading practice provides a base for acquiring the ability to parse sentences in phrases. In silent reading, children can reread sentences in an attempt to understand phrases and experiment with intonation, juncture, and stress. Here the successful readers again have a distinct advantage, since greater amounts of silent reading are assigned to them (Allington, 1982).

Hypothesis 6. Children's different notions about the reading process result in different performances. It may be that poorer readers have developed different theories of reading than successful readers (Canney & Winograd, 1979). Poor readers may view reading as more of an accuracy competition than a meaning-getting exercise; further, they may view it as an activity done to please someone else (Durkin, 1981) and consequently not develop their own response to the activity. With such differences, one might predict that an emphasis on accuracy could, by itself, interfere with the transition to the meaning-oriented phrase-reading stage.

Problems, Strategies, and Promise

A primary problem is the proper role of oral reading fluency in developmental or remedial instruction. While significant evidence suggests that some learners find oral reading difficult and that their lack of fluency interferes with subsequent progress, it is by no means clear that developing oral fluency will help them catch up to the good readers.

Further, the role of oral reading fluency in comprehension is ambiguous. It does seem safe to assert that direct instruction in fluent oral reading produces readers who move from word-by-word reading to a more efficient phrase reading (Chomsky, 1978; Martin & Meltzer, 1976, 1978; Samuels, 1979) and in many cases this training has led to improved reading achievement, usually assessed through some measure of comprehension (Chomsky, 1978; Morgan & Lyon, 1979). Unfortunately, since existing research has rarely been guided by appropriate theory, conclusions about the effects of instruction in oral reading are generally speculative. Yet, oral fluency does seem at least indirectly related to silent reading comprehension, and while a causal relationship has not been adequately demonstrated, Schreiber (1980) argues for such a link and others have demonstrated a correlation between various aspects of oral reading fluency and comprehension (Clay & Imlach, 1971; Dearborn, Johnston, & Carmichael, 1949; Kleiman, Winograd, & Humphrey, 1979; Oaken, Weiner, & Cromer, 1971; Stice, 1978).

Given this, it seems reasonable to provide instruction in fluent oral reading for developing readers who can accurately reproduce words but who read without phrasing or expression. A second problem confronting both the researcher and practitioner is measuring oral reading fluency. While it is not difficult to get high interrater agreement on a "fluent" vs. "not fluent" dichotomy, there exists no efficient scale with demonstrated reliability for quantifying oral reading fluency. Aulls's (1978) method is closest to being desirable, yet is still involves a fair degree of subjectivity. Nonetheless, using an adaptation of Aulls's method (see Table) or simply relying on one's own judgment of fluency is perhaps adequate since we know too little about detailed analyses of fluency.

A third problem concerns how to develop fluency. The articles by Allington (1977, [1983]), Anderson (1980), Chomsky (1978), Cunningham (1979), and Samuels (1979) all contain suggested techniques ranging from repeated readings, read-along, teacher modeling, modified cloze, or greater amounts of silent reading, to reduced teacher monitoring and verbal correction of errors. In addition, Martin and Meltzer (1976, 1978) offer a method that uses computer technology. Although each strategy has promise, some are not readily adaptable to the classroom.

For the daily routine of classroom reading, two strategies seem most applicable. Smith (1979) found that teacher modeling of fluent reading has a positive effect, with minimal class disruption. No special equipment, training, or materials are required. In her study, the teacher simply read aloud the first 100 or so words of each story introduced. The subjects improved their oral reading rate and decreased their errors over the 6-day treatment.

If Hypothesis 1, presented earlier, is correct, the teacher is simply a surrogate for other adult models. Poor readers primarily hear other poor readers in their reading group and rarely have a fluent reading model to emulate. The teacher's modeling, which is probably accompanied by more emphasis on fluency (see Hypothesis 2), seems to produce positive change in oral reading.

A second strategy easily incorporated into the daily routine is repeated readings (Allington, 1977; Cunningham, 1979; Samuels, 1979). In this strategy, the students read the material more than once. Samuels (1979) suggested rereading until a target reading speed is reached (85 wpm).

However, while reading speed is correlated with fluency, the two are not identical. Students in the studies Samuels cites were evidently not given specific fluency instruction but simply required to practice until the criterion rate was

Table Fluency Scale	
Reader reads:	**Score**
word by word.	1
primarily word by word with some 2–3 word phrasing.	2
primarily by phrases (2–3 words) but sometimes word by word; sometimes gives phrases inadequate stress in releation to syntax.	3
primarily in phrases with very little word by word reading; sometimes ignores external punctuation; generally reads in a monotone.	4
primarily in phrases, attending to terminal punctuation; some internal punctuation is ignored; expression is not consistently adequate.	5
in phrases, with fluency, using both terminal and internal punctuation; provides appropriate semantic and syntactic emphasis for purposes of dramatization; expression approximates normal speech.	6

Adapted from FACT: A Multi-Media Reading Program. Richard L. Allington and Steven Brown. Milwaukee, WI: Raintree Publishers, 1979.

reached, a practice-discovery approach. At the reading lab at SUNY-Albany, we have had clinical success over the past 5 years combining instruction and practice. The instruction includes modeling, marking the phrase boundaries lightly in the reading material, and reinforcing successive approximations to fluent reading. Combining this with opportunities to reread material both orally and silently has proven effective in developing improved prosody. We have not required oral reading at first sight, but rather have evaluated oral reading after an initial silent reading.

Intuition guides our application of these strategies. In the future, perhaps research will clarify which methods are most effective with which learners.

Teachers need to consider seriously the value of attending to children's oral reading fluency. Limitations noted aside, a preponderance of empirical and clinical evidence supports the relationship of fluent oral reading and good overall reading ability. Perhaps Schreiber's (1980) argument, that attaining facility in recognizing the unmarked prosodic features of language is central to moving out of word level reading, is a key to improved reading achievement.

Developing oral reading fluency should never become the only goal in beginning or remedial reading instruction, but it is at least as important as many others, e.g., identifying words in isolation or knowing letter–sound correspondences. Developing oral reading fluency is a small step in developing effective and efficient readers, but it is a step in the right direction.

References

Allington, R.L. (1983). The reading instruction provided readers of differing reading abilities. *The Elementary School Journal, 83*(5), 548–559.

Allington, R.L. (1977, October). If they don't read much, how they ever gonna get good? *Journal of Reading, 21*, 57–61.

Allington, R.L. (1980a, November/December). Poor readers don't get to read much in reading groups. *Language Arts, 57*, 872–877.

Allington, R.L. (1980b, June). Teacher interruption behaviors during primary grade oral reading. *Journal of Educational Psychology, 72*, 371–377.

Allington, R.L. (1982, November). *The amount of assigned reading as a fucntion of reader group placement.* Paper presented at the annual conference of the National Council of Teachers of English, Washington, D.C.

Allington, R.L., & Brown, S. (1979). *FACT: A multi-media reading program.* Milwaukee, WI: Raintree.

Alpert, J.L. (1974, June). Teacher behavior across ability groups: A consideration of the mediation of Pygmalion effects. *Journal of Educational Psychology, 66*, 348–353.

Amarel, M., Bussis, A., & Chittenden, E.A. (1977, December). *An approach to the study of beginning reading: Longitudinal case studies.* Paper presented at the National Reading Conference, New Orleans, LA.

Anderson, B. (1980, March). The missing ingredient: Fluent oral reading. *The Elementary School Journal, 81*, 173–178.

Aulls, M.W. (1978). *Developmental and remedial reading.* Boston, MA: Allyn & Bacon.

Aulls, M.W. (1982). *Developing readers in today's elementary school.* Boston, MA: Allyn & Bacon.

Canney, G., & Winograd, P. (1979). *Schemata for reading and reading comprehension performance* (Tech. Rep. No. 120). Urbana, IL: Center for the Study of Reading, University of Illinois.

Cecconi, C.P., Hood, S.B., & Tucker, R.T. (1977, September). Influence of reading level difficulty on the dysfluencies of normal children. *Journal of Speech and Hearing Research, 20*, 455–484.

Chomsky, C. (1978). When you still can't read in third grade: After decoding, what? In S.J. Samuels (Ed.), *What research has to say about reading instruction.* Newark, DE: International Reading Association.

Clay, M. (1979). *Reading: The patterning of complex behavior.* Auckland, New Zealand: Heinemann.

Clay, M., & Imlach, R. (1971, April). Juncture, pitch and stress as reading behavior variables. *Journal of Verbal Learning and Verbal Behavior, 10*, 133–139.

Collins, J. (1982). Discourse style, classroom interaction, and differential treatment. *Journal of Reading Behavior, 14*, 326–341.

Cunningham, J.W. (1979, January). An automatic pilot for decoding. *The Reading Teacher, 32*, 420–424.

Dahl, P.R., & Samuels, S.J. (1974). *A mastery based experimental program for teaching poor readers high speed word recognition skills.* Unpublished paper, University of Minnesota, Minneapolis.

Dearborn, W.F., Johnston, P.W., & Carmichael, L. (1949, October). Oral stress and the meaning of printed words. *Science, 110*, 404.

deVilliers, J.G., & deVilliers, P.A. (1978). *Language acquisition.* Cambridge, MA: Harvard University Press.

Durkin, D. (1974–1975). A six-year study of children who learned to read in school at the age of four. *Reading Research Quarterly, 10*, 9–61.

Durkin, D. (1981). Reading comprehension instruction in five basal reader series. *Reading Research Quarterly, 16*, 515–544.

Gambrell, L.B., Wilson, R.B., & Gantt, W.N. (1981, July–August). Classroom observations of task-attending behaviors of good and poor readers. *Journal of Educational Research, 74,* 400–404.

Jorgenson, G.W. (1977, February). Relationship of classroom behavior to the accuracy of the match between material difficulty and student ability. *Journal of Educational Psychology, 69,* 24–32.

Kleiman, G.M., Winograd, P.N., & Humphrey, M.H. (1979). *Prosody and children's parsing of sentences* (Tech. Rep. No. 123). Urbana, IL: Center for the Study of Reading, University of Illinois.

LaBerge, D., & Samuels, S.J. (1974). Toward a theory of automatic information processing in reading. *Cognitive Psychology, 6,* 293–323.

Martin, J.G., & Meltzer, R.H. (1976, Fall). Visual rhythms: Report on a method for facilitating the teaching of reading. *Journal of Reading Behavior, 8,* 153–160.

Martin, J.G., & Meltzer, R.H. (1978). Visual rhythms: Dynamic text display for learning to read a second language. *Visible Language, 12,* 71–80.

Morgan, R., & Lyon, E. (1979). Paired reading: A preliminary report on a technique for parental tuition of reading retarded children. *Journal of Child Psychology and Psychiatry, 20,* 151–160.

Neville, M.H. (1968, October). Effects of oral and echoic responses in beginning reading. *Journal of Educational Psychology, 59,* 362–369.

Oaken, R., Weiner, M., & Cromer, W. (1971, February). Identification, organization and reading comprehension for good and poor readers. *Journal of Educational Psychology, 62,* 71–78.

Resnick, L.B. (1970, October). Relations between perceptual and syntactic control in oral reading. *Journal of Educational Psychology, 61,* 382–385.

Rubin, R.A. (1975, March). Reading ability and assigned materials: Accommodation for the slow but not for the accelerated. *The Elementary School Journal, 75,* 373–377.

Samuels, S.J. (1979, January). The method of repeated readings. *The Reading Teacher, 32,* 403–408.

Schreiber, P.A. (1980, Fall). On the acquisition of reading fluency. *Journal of Reading Behavior, 12,* 177–186.

Smith, D.D. (1979, March). The improvement of children's oral reading through the use of teacher modeling. *Journal of Learning Disabilities, 12,* 39–42.

Stice, C.K. (1978, May). The relationship between comprehension of oral contrastive stress and silent reading comprehension. *Research in the Teaching of English, 12,* 137–142.

Weinstein, R.S. (1976, February). Reading group membership in first grade: Teacher behaviors and pupil experience over time. *Journal of Educational Psychology, 68,* 103–116.

Questions for Reflection

• Try evaluating the oral reading of some of your students using the Fluency Scale presented in the table. In general, do your students read with appropriate speed and prosody? If not, how can you build time into your schedule to allow them time to practice meaningful with oral reading?

• How often do you read aloud to your students? How often do your colleagues working at different grade levels read aloud? How much oral reading do you think benefits students of different ages? Could your students benefit from more opportunities to listen to you reading aloud?

• Consider your own oral reading. What can you do to make sure that you are providing students with the most effective modeling possible? How can you evaluate your own prosody, speed, phrasing, and so on? Do you ever practice reading aloud before doing so in class?

• Author Richard Allington asks, Given that recent research has shown that extensive independent reading works as well as or better than the repeated readings technique, are your students with fluency problems doing sufficient independent reading both in school and out? Do you have ideas about how to increase the amount of independent reading the students do?

Fluency for Everyone: Incorporating Fluency Instruction in the Classroom

Timothy V. Rasinski

Although there is no universal agreement about what constitutes reading fluency, most authorities would agree that it refers to the smooth and natural oral production of text.

Harris and Hodges (1981), for example, define fluency as expressing oneself "smoothly, easily, and readily," having "freedom from word identification problems," and dealing with "words, and larger language units" with quickness (p. 120). Thus, at a minimum one might expect the fluent reader to read orally with accuracy, quickness, and expression.

Achieving fluency is recognized as an important aspect of proficient reading, but it remains a neglected goal of reading instruction (Allington, 1983). Most basal reading programs give little recognition to fluency as an important goal, and few reading textbooks for prospective teachers provide an in-depth treatment of the topic.

Reading fluency often becomes a salient issue only when students demonstrate deficiencies. These students are often referred to corrective or remedial classes where they finally receive special instruction in the development of fluent reading.

How can classroom teachers teach fluency to their students? Several methods have been proven successful. These include repeated readings (Dowhower, 1987; Herman, 1985; Samuels, 1979), reading while listening or echo reading (Carbo, 1978; Chomsky, 1976; Gamby, 1983; Laffey & Kelly, 1981; Schneeberg, 1977; Van Der Leij, 1981), the neurological impress method (Heckelman, 1969), and reading in phrases (Allington, 1983; Amble & Kelly, 1970; Gregory, 1986).

One potential problem with these fluency training methods is that they were, in general, originally intended for use in corrective reading situations involving an instructor working with one, two, or a very small group of students. Despite many positive aspects of these methods, the focus of their application is overly narrow.

Teachers who wish to make fluency instruction an integral part of the regular reading curriculum may be at a loss in attempting to use corrective fluency methods in a way that is appropriate for the more normal reader.

Fortunately, the methods show to be effective in helping less fluent readers suggest a set of principles that teachers may find helpful. In the remainder of this article those principles will be identified and discussed.

Proven Methods

Repetition. Achieving fluency requires practice with one text until a criterion level is achieved.

Although the principle of repetition is often translated into repeated exposures to target words in isolation, research has shown that repetition is most effective when students meet the target words in a variety of texts or through repeated exposures to one text.

Although repetition of texts may seem to be a dull activity, there are several ways to make it interesting and appealing. For example, young

Reprinted from Rasinski, T.V. (1989). Fluency for everyone: Incorporating fluency instruction in the classroom. *The Reading Teacher, 42*(9), 690–693.

children love to hear their favorite stories read to them repeatedly (Beaver, 1982) and students enjoy working in pairs on repeated reading tasks (Koskinen & Blum, 1986).

Rasinski (1988) suggests several ways to use natural classroom events to encourage repeated readings. Activities such as putting on plays and having older students read short books to primary students require that students practice the text they will have to perform later on.

Model. Young students and other less fluent readers may not always know what fluent reading should be like. Poor readers, for example, are usually assigned to reading groups in which the predominant model of reading is other disfluent readers. It seems clear that students need frequent opportunities to see and hear fluent reading.

Since the most fluent reader in the classroom is the teacher, the teacher should be the primary model. The easiest and most stimulating way to do this is to read good children's literature to the class. Daily periods should be set aside for teachers (and other fluent readers) to read aloud.

Direct instruction and feedback. Research into metacognition in reading is demonstrating that it may be important for readers to be aware of what happens when they read and why they have reading problems. This awareness may be particularly helpful in the development of fluency.

Prior to reading aloud, the teacher could remind the class to listen to the expression in his/her voice during the reading, the speed at which the text is read, or when stops or pauses occur. A short discussion of these factors after the reading or before students' own oral reading could heighten students' sensitivity to their own reading.

Similarly, providing feedback to students after they read orally can facilitate growth in fluent reading. Koskinen and Blum (1986), for example, propose a model of instruction in which students are trained to provide feedback to each other. The reader benefits from a formative critique of his or her reading and the student critic benefits from a heightened metacognitive sense of what it means to be a fluent reader.

Support during reading. The notion of scaffolding or support while performing is critical to the development of fluency, especially in the beginning stages or with students having difficulty. Support is achieved through the student hearing a fluent rendition of a passage while simultaneously reading the same. Several types of support are available.

Choral reading is perhaps the most common form of support reading and is highly appropriate for the regular classroom. Here students read a selected passage in unison. The teacher needs to ensure that several fluent readers are part of the group or that his/her own voice leads the way in the choral reading.

The neurological impress method (Heckelman, 1969) was designed as a remedial technique for use one to one. The teacher begins by reading slightly ahead of and louder than the student, and later, as the student gains in fluency, softly shadows the student's reading of the passage. Although labor intensive, the technique can be adapted for regular classroom use with aides, volunteers, or fluent classmates.

The use of tape recorded passages is another way to provide support during reading. Carbo (1978) reported students making good progress in reading while simultaneously listening to passages on tape. This format is especially appealing as it allows students to work on their fluency independently. They may need to be reminded to concentrate on reading the passage, not simply listen passively to it.

Text unit. Fluency involves reading texts in multiword chunks or phrases. Word by word reading, even if it is accurate and fast, is not fluent reading. Timely reminders should help drive the point home.

Research has shown (e.g., Weiss, 1983) that marking phrase boundaries in student texts with a penciled slash or vertical line may aid fluency. Occasionally reading short texts such as poems, famous speeches, or popular songs marked in this way may help students develop and maintain a mature sense of phrasing.

Easy materials. Fluency is best promoted when students are provided with materials that they find relatively easy in terms of word recognition, so that they can move beyond decoding to issues of phrasing, expression, and comprehensibility of production. These materials help students develop a sense of power and confidence.

Teachers, then, need to stock their classroom libraries with books that represent a variety of difficulty levels and interests. For their independent reading, students can be directed to those materials that they will not find frustrating.

Combining Principles

These principles offer some building blocks and guidelines for developing reading instruction and activities that promote the development of fluency. Rather than think of them in isolation, teachers can design lessons and activities that combine two or more of these principles.

In her study of disfluent third graders, Carol Chomsky (1976) combined the principles of repetition and support. She had students listen to and read a tape recorded text until they could read it with fluency. Then they received instruction in various components of the text.

In a similar vein Koskinen and Blum's (1986) instructional model for fluency combines repetition and direct instruction. Students read a text three times and receive formative feedback (direct instruction in fluency) from their peers. In both the Chomsky and Koskinen and Blum models, students made substantial improvements in fluency.

Hoffman (1987) and Aulls (1982) offer even more complex models of fluency instruction which combine elements of modeling, repetition, support, and direct instruction.

Teachers Empowered

The point is not that teachers should blindly endorse any of the models identified and described here. Rather, relying upon the principles of fluency instruction, informed and creative teachers can design instructional activities that meet the unique needs of their classrooms. They can incorporate one or more principles into the stories that students encounter in their daily lessons or pleasure reading, and depending upon students' progress can employ principles more or less strenuously.

Fluency is an issue that needs to be taken seriously in the reading classroom. The principles outlined here, while neither prescriptive nor panacea, offer teachers several tools for making their reading instruction reflect their own professional judgment.

Through the use of principles such as these, prepackaged and "teacher proof" reading programs that foster deskilling and promote a perception of teachers as incompetent can be turned back in favor of alternative and effective teacher designed instruction.

References

Allington, R.L. (1983, February). Fluency: The neglected reading goal. *The Reading Teacher, 36*, 556–561.

Amble, B.R., & Kelly, F.J. (1970). Phrase reading development training with fourth grade students: An experimental and comparative study. *Journal of Reading Behavior, 2*(1), 85–96.

Aulls, M.W. (1982). *Developing readers in today's elementary school*. Boston: Allyn & Bacon.

Beaver, J.M. (1982, February). Say it! Over and over. *Language Arts, 59*, 143–148.

Carbo, M. (1978, December). Teaching reading with talking books. *The Reading Teacher, 32*, 267–273.

Chomsky, C. (1976, March). After decoding: What? *Language Arts, 53*, 288–296.

Dowhower, S.L. (1987). Effects of repeated reading on second-grade transitional readers' fluency and comprehension. *Reading Research Quarterly, 22*(4), 389–406.

Gamby, G. (1983, January). Talking books and taped books. *The Reading Teacher, 36*, 366–369.

Gregory, J.F. (1986). Phrasing in the speech and reading of the hearing impaired. *Journal of Communication Disorders, 19*(4), 289–297.

Harris, T.L., & Hodges, R.E. (Eds.). (1981). *A dictionary of reading*. Newark, DE: International Reading Association.

Heckelman, R.G. (1969, Summer). A neurological impress method of reading instruction. *Academic Therapy, 4*, 277–282.

Herman, P.A. (1985, Fall). The effect of repeated readings on reading rate, speech pauses, and word recognition accuracy. *Reading Research Quarterly, 20*, 553–564.

Hoffman, J.V. (1987). Rethinking the role of oral reading in basal instruction. *The Elementary School Journal, 87*(3), 367–373.

Koskinen, P., & Blum, I. (1986, October). Paired repeated reading: A classroom strategy for developing fluent reading. *The Reading Teacher, 40*, 70–75.

Laffey, J.L., & Kelly, D. (1981). Repeated reading of taped literature: Does it make a difference? In G. McNinch

(Ed.), *Comprehension: Process and change* (first year-book of the American Reading Forum). Hattiesburg: University of Southern Mississippi Press.

Rasinski, T.V. (1988, July). Making repeated readings a functional part of classroom reading instruction. *Reading Horizons, 28*, 250–254.

Samuels, S.J. (1979, January). The method of repeated readings. *The Reading Teacher, 32*, 403–408.

Schneeberg, H. (1977, March). Listening while reading: A four year study. *The Reading Teacher, 30*, 629–635.

Van Der Leij, A. (1981). Remediation of reading-disabled children by presenting text simultaneously to eye and ear. *Bulletin of the Orton Society, 31*, 229–243.

Weiss, D.S. (1983). The effects of text segmentation on children's reading comprehension. *Discourse Processes, 6*(1), 77–89.

Questions for Reflection

• The author suggests several ways in which students can be enlisted to help one another in gaining fluency—from older students reading to younger children to peers' provision of feedback on oral reading performance. Think about the students in your class. How could you encourage them to work together to improve fluency? Now think beyond your classroom. Do you have colleagues you could work with to establish cross-age tutoring or other approaches to expand the support available for students?

• Repeated reading of the same text is a popular approach that provides the practice needed for students to develop fluency. As the author points out, it is important that the texts used for repeated reading be at an appropriate level so that readers' attention is not overly focused on decoding. Take a look at your classroom library. Do you have a good collection of texts at a variety of levels, of different genres, and about a range of topics to engage the children in your class? Do you have access to a librarian in your school or district who might be able to assist with recommendations or ideas for expanding your collection? How do you determine which texts are right for which children? How do you help children with their own choices of which texts to read? In what ways can you make repeated readings an authentic experience for students, so they are not practicing simply to increase their reading speed?

The Method of Repeated Readings

S. Jay Samuels

A mentally retarded elementary school student asks for a stopwatch for his birthday so that he can keep track of his gains in reading speed with each rereading of short paragraphs he has selected. An adult with a history of reading failure continues to reread a passage after her tutor has left because for the first time she is reading with fluency. In a junior high school remedial reading classroom, a group of students wearing earphones is rereading a story while simultaneously listening to it on a tape recorder.

These situations share a little known and easily used technique called the method of repeated readings. Some teachers are familiar with this technique and have used it, but it is so useful for building reading fluency that it deserves to be more widely known and used.

It is important to point out that repeated reading is not a method for teaching all beginning reading skills. Rather, it is intended as a supplement in a developmental reading program. While the method is particularly suitable for students with special learning problems, it is useful for normal children as well.

While we were researching this method at the University of Minnesota, unknown to us Carol Chomsky at Harvard University was using similar techniques with poor readers and was getting similar good results. With regard to the effectiveness of this method, she (Chomsky 1978) states, "The procedure proved to be facilitating for slow and halting readers, increasing fluency rapidly and with apparent ease. Successive stories required fewer listenings to reach fluency.... The work provided in addition a heightened sense of confidence and motivation. Within several months the children become far more willing and able to undertake reading new material on their own."

What Is the Procedure?

The method consists of rereading a short, meaningful passage several times until a satisfactory level of fluency is reached. Then the procedure is repeated with a new passage.

For example, in one of our earlier studies, children who had been experiencing great difficulty in learning to read were instructed to select easy stories which were of interest to them. Then, depending on the reading skill of the student, short selections (50–200 words) from these stories were marked off for practice.

The student read the short selection to an assistant, who recorded the reading speed and number of word recognition errors on a graph, as shown in the Figure. The student then returned to his/her seat and practiced reading the selection while the next student read to the assistant. When the first student's turn came again, the procedure was repeated until an 85-word-per-minute criterion rate was reached. Then the student went on to the next passage.

The accompanying Figure shows the progress made by one student on reading speed and word recognition accuracy on five separate passages. These passages began at tests 1, 8, 15, 21, and 25. As reading speed increased, word recognition errors decreased. As the student continued to use this technique, the initial speed of reading each new selection was faster than initial speed on the previous selection. Also, the number of rereadings required to reach the criterion

Reprinted from Samuels, S.J. (1997). The method of repeated readings. *The Reading Teacher*, 50(5), 376–381. (Published originally in *The Reading Teacher*, vol. 32, January 1979, and updated for the 1997 reprinting reproduced here.)

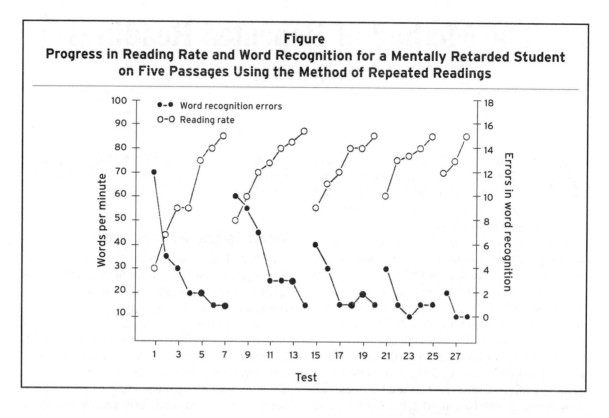

Figure
Progress in Reading Rate and Word Recognition for a Mentally Retarded Student on Five Passages Using the Method of Repeated Readings

reading speed decreased as the student continued the technique.

The fact that starting rates were faster with each new selection and fewer rereadings were necessary to reach goals indicates transfer of training and a general improvement in reading fluency. Although this figure shows the progress of one individual, the charts for other students were quite similar.

Since the main purpose of repeated reading is to build fluency, it is important to be able to define fluency in ways which are observable and measurable. In the Minnesota research, fluency was separated into two components—accuracy of word recognition and reading speed. While both components are important, for purposes of building fluency, speed was emphasized.

Why emphasize speed over accuracy? There appears to be a trade-off between accuracy and speed. If 100% word recognition accuracy is required before the student can move on to a new passage, the student becomes fearful of making a mistake, and consequently the pace of reading

slows down. In fact, if we overemphasize accuracy, we tend to impede fluency. Therefore, for purposes of building fluency, speed rather than accuracy should be stressed.

Repeated readings can be done either with or without audio support. If audio support is used, the student reads the passage silently while listening to the tape recorded narration over earphones. After a number of rereadings, the audio support is no longer necessary and the student reads the story without help.

There are additional factors to consider regarding the use of repeated readings. So that students will understand why rereading is done, we have involved them in a discussion of how athletes develop skill at their sports. This discussion brings out the fact that athletes spend considerable time practicing basic skills until they develop speed and smoothness at their activity. Repeated readings uses this same type of practice.

Some teachers who are considering using repeated readings are concerned that the method will lead to student boredom. On the contrary, we found that the students were excited by the gains they made in fluency. Similarly, Amarel (1978) has found that beginning readers are very interested in working at the skills necessary for helping them to comprehend text.

While it is not essential that each student keep an individual reading record of the type in the Figure, we found it to be an excellent motivating device. Without the graph, gains can at times go unnoticed. The graph provides visible proof of progress. Of course, a tape recording can show improvement from an early to a later reading and is useful for showing gains in fluency to students and their parents.

What About Comprehension?

Teachers may wonder what role comprehension plays in the rereading method. Repeated reading is a meaningful task in that the students are reading interesting material in context. Comprehension may be poor with the first reading of the text, but with each additional rereading, the student is better able to comprehend because the decoding barrier to comprehension is gradually overcome. As less attention is required for decoding, more attention becomes available for comprehension. Thus rereading both builds fluency and enhances comprehension. One additional technique for building comprehension is to ask the student a different comprehension question with each rereading of the story.

The amount of material to be read depends on the student's skill. Generally the passage should be short. At Minnesota our early experimental work was done with mentally retarded students without audio support. These students had extremely poor reading skills, and we started them on passages of about 50 words. As they gained in reading skills, the length of the passages increased to 200 words.

In other studies, students of average intelligence who were word-by-word readers were given passages of about 200 words. These passages usually came from a book the student had selected, which was broken into short passages. Once mastery on one short passage was reached, the next short section of the book was used for

practice. By breaking a longer story into parts and mastering one part at a time before moving on, the student experiences relatively frequent successes.

Other students in the class, teacher aides, and parents can be used to help with repeated readings. They can listen to students read, record word recognition errors and time, and help with words the students need to learn. In other words, while the teacher is giving directed reading instruction to one group of students, other students, either on their own or with the aid of others, can be practicing repeated readings.

Theoretical Rationale

The rereading method emerged largely from the teaching implications of the theory of automatic information processing in reading (LaBerge & Samuels, 1974). According to automaticity theory, a fluent reader decodes text automatically—that is, without attention—thus leaving attention free to be used for comprehension. Beginning readers, on the other hand, are nonautomatic in their decoding since attention is required. Because the beginning reader's attention is on decoding, it is not immediately available for comprehension, thus making the process of deriving meaning more difficult and slower.

In approaching the problem of how teachers can help students develop fluent reading skills, we traced the development of word recognition skill through its three levels. The first level is what may be called the nonaccurate stage. The student has great difficulty in recognizing words, even when a reasonable amount of time is provided.

The next level is the accuracy stage. The student is able to recognize printed words with accuracy but attention is required. When listening to the oral reading of a student who is at the accuracy stage, one notes that the reading is rather slow and halting, without expression, and despite high word recognition accuracy, there may be poor comprehension.

The third and most advanced level is what we call the automatic stage. At the automatic stage, the student is able to recognize the printed words without attention. The oral reading of a student at the automatic stage is characterized by a rate which approximates or may even be faster than speaking rate, the reading is with expression, and if the material is familiar, the student should be able to comprehend while reading aloud.

Currently we do not have tests suitable for classroom use which would tell us if a student is at the automaticity stage, so we have to settle for what may be called indicators of automaticity. Fortunately, several research studies suggest that speed of response may be used as an indicator of automaticity (LaBerge, 1973; Perfetti & Lesgold, n.d.; McCormick & Samuels, 1976).

Teachers can do two things to help students achieve automaticity in word recognition. They can give instruction on how to recognize words at the accuracy level. Second, they can provide the time and the motivation so that the student will practice these word recognition skills until they become automatic. One important function of repeated reading is that it provides the practice needed to become automatic.

Several other questions had to be dealt with in the development of the project. Are there activities in which extremely high levels of performance are required? If there are such activities, are the methods of training different from those used in teaching reading? The answers to these questions led directly to the development of repeated reading.

Compare With Music, Sports

Two general areas in which high levels of performance are required come immediately to mind: sports and music. In sports such as football, soccer, boxing, and wrestling, moves must be made rapidly and automatically.

Musicianship is somewhat different from sports but bears many similarities to reading. The musician is faced with a text comprised of notes. The goal is not just the mechanical rendition of sounds indicated by the notes, but rather the rendering of those printed notes with fluency and expression. Decoding must be done automatically so that the mind of the musician is free to play the score with emotion and feeling.

When comparing the methods used to train athletes and musicians to those used in reading, one notes an important difference. Both in athletics and music, the beginning student is given a small unit of activity and this unit is practiced over and over until it is mastered. At the risk of overgeneralizing, in contrast, we in reading are often too eager to have children cover a year's work in a year's time, so that some children, especially those having difficulty with reading, are moved too rapidly through a book, never having mastered a single page. What repeated readings does is to give the student the opportunity to master the material before moving on.

Leaving the theoretical side of repeated reading, let us examine how versions of this method were used in early schooling. In 17th-century America and Europe, the books used for reading instruction frequently contained familiar material, some of which the student could recite from memory but could not read. For example, hornbooks, used in 17th-century America, introduced reading through the use of prayers and verses already familiar to the children (Meyer, 1957, p. 34). Common prayers were also included in *The New England Primer* (Ford, 1899, p. 13).

Another text used frequently for teaching reading was the catechism (Littlefield, 1904, p. 106). Young Puritans memorized the catechism at home, and later at school reading was taught by having them read from the catechism. In Europe, school was often taught by the local priest, who integrated memorization of the catechism with reading.

Small (1914, p. 366) reports the Bible was one of the most popular texts. In a religious age, many of the Bible stories were already familiar to the young children. The teacher would then have skilled readers repeatedly read the same Bible passage orally until the less skilled had learned the words

In each of the cases mentioned, the children were introduced to reading with material which was known to them, and they read the material a number of times until they were able to read the words with some degree of fluency.

Recent reports of methods used by Heckelman (1969) and Hollingsworth (1970) superficially resemble repeated reading. Their "listening while reading" technique attempts to increase reading fluency in slow readers. However, their students read new material at each listening session instead of concentrating on a particular passage until mastery was reached.

Recent studies using repeated reading have produced interesting results. Gonzales and Elijah (1975) had students who were at the third grade reading level read the same passage twice. The researchers found that the second reading had 3.3% fewer errors than the first reading. This improvement was equivalent to the second reading's being at the instructional level of difficulty whereas the first reading was at the frustration level.

In another study, Terry (1974) had college students read *Reader's Digest* stories typed in mirror-image print. She reported that while the first reading was painfully slow with poor comprehension for most students, both speed and accuracy improved following several readings. After a week of repeated reading practice using a new story each day, the comprehension rate was as high as it was for stories typed in regular print.

It should be pointed out in closing that a carefully designed empirical study of repeated readings (Dahl & Samuels, n.d.) was done with elementary school children who were the poorest readers in the school but who were of normal intelligence. When repeated readings were used as an adjunct to regular instruction, significant gains were made over the control group in both comprehension and reading speed.

The theoretical and empirical evidence in this article leads us to believe that the method of repeated readings deserves to be more widely used as a technique for building fluency in reading.

Author Notes

I was very pleased to learn that my article on repeated reading, published almost 20 years ago, is being reissued. Since its publication, I have kept a literature search on this topic and have learned the following from the almost 200 studies on the topic:

1. The original finding has been replicated; that is, a high degree of accuracy and speed develops on the practiced text. We can give accuracy and speed another name if we wish—fluency.

2. There is transfer of fluency to other portions of the text, even the parts that were not specifically practiced. Some have even reported improvements in comprehension.

3. Repeated reading is the most universally used remedial reading technique to help poor readers achieve reading skill.

4. Repeated reading is now widely used to teach reading in foreign languages.

References
Amarel, M. (1978). Educational Testing Service reading study. *Institute for Research in Teaching: Notes and News, 5*, 2–3.

Chomsky, C. (1978). When you still can't read in third grade: After decoding, what? In S.J. Samuels (Ed.), *What research has to say about reading instruction* (pp. 13–30). Newark, DE: International Reading Association.

Dahl, P.R., & Samuels, S.J. (n.d.). *A mastery based experimental program for teaching poor readers high speed word recognition skills.* Unpublished manuscript.

Ford, P.L. (1899). *The New England primer.* New York: Dodd, Mead.

Gonzales, P.G., & Elijah, D.V. (1975). Rereading: Effect on error patterns and performance levels on the IRI. *The Reading Teacher, 28*, 647–652.

Heckelman, R.G. (1969). A neurological impress method of reading instruction. *Academic Therapy, 44*, 277–282.

Hollingsworth, P.M. (1970). An experiment with the impress method of teaching reading. *The Reading Teacher, 24*, 112–114.

LaBerge, D. (1973). Attention and the measurement of perceptual learning. *Memory and Cognition. 1*, 268–276.

LaBerge, D., & Samuels , S.J. (1974). Toward a theory of automatic information processing in reading. *Cognitive Psychology, 6*, 293–323.

Littlefield, G.E. (1904). *Early schools and schoolbooks of New England.* Boston: The Club of Odd Volumes.

McCormick, C., & Samuels, S.J. (1976). *Word recognition by second graders: The unit of perception and interrelationships among accuracy, latency and comprehension* (Research Rep. No. 102). Minneapolis, MN: Research,

Development and Demonstration Center in Education of Handicapped Children, University of Minnesota.

Meyer, A.E. (1957). *An educational history of the American people*. New York: McGraw-Hill.

Perfetti, C., & Lesgold, A. (n.d.). *Coding and comprehension in skilled reading*. Unpublished manuscript, University of Pittsburgh, PA.

Small, W.H. (1914). *Early New England schools*. Boston: Ginn.

Terry, P. (1974). *The effect of orthographic transformations upon speed and accuracy of semantic categorization*. Unpublished doctoral dissertation, University of Minnesota, Minneapolis.

Questions for Reflection

• The author mentions that teachers new to the method of repeated readings express concern about the potential for student boredom. If you have used the method, what has been your experience? How can you ensure that students remain engaged when doing repeated readings?

• Consider the author's explanation for why speed is emphasized over accuracy. Do you agree with his observation that overemphasis on accuracy tends to discourage readers, who then read more slowly and less fluently? At what point would you think that accuracy should gain attention?

• In his notes, included with the 1997 reprinting of the original 1979 article, the author indicates that repeated readings are frequently used with students learning a foreign language. Do you think the method would be helpful for English-language learners? Would it need to be adapted in any way for use with these students in contrast to struggling learners who speak English as a native language?

Paired Repeated Reading: A Classroom Strategy for Developing Fluent Reading

Patricia S. Koskinen and Irene H. Blum

In characterizing the acquisition of skilled reading, Allington (1977, 1980, 1983), Downing (1982), and Smith (1982) emphasize the critical importance of having many opportunities to *read* and the role of practice in developing fluency. The recently published report of the U.S. National Commission on Reading expresses a similar view. *Becoming a Nation of Readers* (Anderson et al., 1985) synthesizes a considerable body of research on the reading process, environmental influences on reading, and teaching techniques, tools, and testing. They suggest that "Reading, like playing a musical instrument, is not something that is mastered once and for all at a certain age. Rather, it is a skill that continues to improve through practice" (p. 16). The report recommends that the best form of practice involves the "whole skill of reading," or reading natural, meaningful text (p. 17).

Research findings have consistently agreed that the amount of time spent reading is an important variable in reading achievement (Allington, 1980, 1983; Durkin, 1978–1979; Hiebert, 1983). Yet, following extensive observations, Durkin (1978–1979) concluded that very little reading goes on in instruction beyond what is required to complete assignments. Similarly, Gambrell (1984) reported that, during teacher directed instruction, primary grade students are engaged in reading contextual materials (rather than isolated words and sentences) for only 2 to 5 minutes daily.

Providing sufficient time and experiences with contextual materials during reading instruction may be particularly important for students who are having difficulty learning to read. These students seldom read when it is not required. Yet, good readers consistently have more opportunities to read contextual materials in instruction than do poor readers (Allington, 1977, 1980, 1983; Gambrell, Wilson, & Gantt, 1981).

Recently, there has been considerable interest in a variety of repeated reading strategies and their role in developing skilled fluent reading. Researchers using these strategies, which provide substantial practice in reading contextual materials repeatedly, have well documented evidence of improved fluency and word recognition and indications of enhanced comprehension in individualized settings (Blum & Koskinen, 1982; Chomsky, 1976; Herman, 1985; Herman, Dewitz, & Stammer, 1980; O'Shea, Sindelar, & O'Shea, 1985; Samuels, 1979; Taylor, Wade, & Yekovich, 1985).

A repetition strategy has also been effective in classrooms. When teachers used paired repeated reading (an adaptation of repeated reading) as part of regular reading instruction, significant differences were found in its favor in both oral fluency and comprehension (Koskinen & Blum, 1984).

How Paired Repeated Reading Works

Paired repeated reading enables classroom teachers to use repeated reading with a minimum of management difficulties. This strategy gives beginning readers or older students with reading

Reprinted from Koskinen, P.S., & Blum, I.H. (1986). Paired repeated reading: A classroom strategy for developing fluent reading. *The Reading Teacher, 40*(1), 70–75.

difficulties an opportunity to read contextual materials a number of times so they can experience fluent reading.

While paired repeated reading can be used in many ways, a typical activity takes 10 to 15 minutes and is done with a partner from the reading group during independent follow up to reading instruction. Students read a short passage aloud three times and then evaluate their own and their partner's reading. Many types of reading material can be used, such as passages from basal readers, student produced stories, or trade books.

When used as part of the regular classroom reading program, paired repeated reading involves the following steps:

1. The students each select their own passage from material they are currently using in instruction, counting out approximately 50 words. Having students select different passages makes listening to a partner read more interesting and discourages direct comparison of reading proficiency.

2. Students read their passages silently and then decide who will be the first reader.

3. Reader: This student reads his/her passage aloud to a partner three different times. Readers may ask their partner for help with a word. After each oral reading, the reader answers the question "How well did you read?" on a self evaluation sheet.

   Listener: This student listens to his/her partner read and, after the second and third reading, tells the partner how his/her reading improved and notes this improvement on a "listening" sheet.

4. After the third reading, students switch roles, and again follow Step 3.

Teaching the Strategy

Students enjoy paired repeated reading, and they quickly learn to do it without direct teacher supervision. Many teachers who have used this strategy say students can use it independently after a brief introduction. To insure success,

students need to understand (1) the procedures for repeated reading, (2) how to listen carefully to a partner and make positive comments on reading improvement, and (3) how to select material for repeated reading. Teachers find that if they introduce these ideas to a reading group and then provide supervised practice, independent use of the strategy comes very easily.

The following three session introduction has been particularly effective.

Session 1: Learning the Role of the Reader

Students need a chance to practice just the role of the reader. Tell them they will be reading a short passage several times so that they can get better and better at reading it. An analogy such as basketball players shooting foul shots over and over to improve their skills can help students understand the value of practice.

Have students work in pairs, each reading a different short (25 word) passage from their group's current reading material. Have them all read their material silently and then have one of the pair read their passage to a partner.

When students have finished reading their passage once, introduce an evaluation sheet which has the question "How well did you read?" written three different times. Show students how to respond after each oral reading to a Likert-type scale ranging from "fantastic" to "terrible." (See Figure 1.)

Students who have just read aloud can mark the evaluation sheet and then read the passage two more times, evaluating each of the successive readings. Supervise students until all have had a chance to do paired repeated readings.

Session 2: Learning the Role of the Listener

The teacher needs to model the role of the listener. Mention to students that the listeners in paired repeated reading can really help their partner, not only by telling words if asked, but also by pointing out how reading has improved. Give students practice in listening for

Figure 1
Sample Portion of "Dog Gone Good" Reading Sheet

Reading # 1
How well did you read

| fantastic | good | fair | not so good | terrible |

Dog drawings selected from *Reading Attitude Inventory*, P. Cambell, Livonia Public Schools, Livonia, Michigan, 1966.

Figure 2
Sample Portion of "Dog Gone Good" Listening Sheet

Reading #3
How did your partner's reading get better?

He or she read more smoothly?
He or she knew more words
He or she read with more expression

★ Tell your partner one thing that was better about his or her reading.

---

improvement by first reading a few sentences in a halting monotone or with many errors, and then reading the same sentences again with expression or with fewer mispronunciations. Develop with students a list of ways the second reading improved.

To help students focus on listening, give them a "listening" sheet to use during their partner's second and third reading. Suggest responses to the question "How did your partner get better?" such as "_____ read more smooth," "_____ knew more words," or "_____ read with more expression." (See Figure 2.) In addition to marking their sheet, listeners are to tell their partner how he/she improved.

Supervise students while they practice doing paired repeated reading in both the listening and reading roles.

Session 3: Putting It Together

The third session is to acquaint students with procedures for selecting passages to read and provide one final supervised paired practice. Show students how to select different short passages approximately 50 words in length, being sure to end at a complete sentence. Supervise them as they do the entire paired repeated reading procedure, including the self evaluation and listening sheets. Be sure that students answer the self evaluation question after each reading, and the listener gives a positive comment after the partner's second or third reading.

Classroom Management Tips

Paired repeated reading provides students with practice in reading segments of meaningful text in a setting which requires limited teacher supervision. After students have been introduced to the strategy and have had supervised practice, they can use this strategy during their independent assignment time. Here are a few tips for independent classroom use.

1. Select Short Interesting Passages

Since pairs of students will read passages three times each, short passages (50 to 75 words) insure an activity not longer than 10 to 15 minutes. With longer passages, the listener and reader may become less attentive. As students become aware of their audience, encourage them to select passages that are especially appropriate for oral reading.

2. Be Sure Material Is at the Reader's Independent Level

One purpose of repeated reading is to give the reader the feeling of fluent reading. The material should be at a level where mastery is possible. Anything that students can read independently, such as a basal reader or language experience story which has been discussed already in class, is appropriate. If the material is too difficult, students become frustrated, are not attentive to the task, or disturb others by asking a variety of classmates for help.

3. Encourage Attentive Listening

Teachers find that having a student be an active listener has many benefits. Having an audience motivates the reader, and the listener learns to notice aspects that make for better reading. Providing the listener with a purpose (giving positive comments on improvement) and a structured format (the listening sheet) help keep the listener on task.

The listening role was developed initially to keep partners involved, but one of the unplanned benefits has been the pleasure readers experience from hearing compliments about their reading. Many readers, especially those experiencing difficulty, have seldom received praise for their reading and almost never have gotten compliments

from their friends. Teachers also find that monitoring a partner's reading helps students monitor their own reading as well.

4. Provide Guidelines for Working in Pairs

Since cooperative learning has so many benefits, providing opportunities and guidelines is important. Guidance in getting down to work immediately, checking with each other on the purpose of the task, taking turns, and voice modulation should all be discussed. A 2 minute practice session on using different voice levels—such as one for speaking to a whole class, another for a reading group, and still another for speaking to a person right next to you—can help students become aware of the noise level.

There is no one way to pair students. Try different types, such as same sex, teacher assigned, student choice, and monitor the changing of pairs so that variety and harmony are present.

Students need to know that working with a partner is a privilege, not a right, and they earn it by following the class guidelines. If a few overstep the boundaries, have them work independently for a while and then join students working in pairs for another try at cooperative learning.

Because working in pairs often makes learning particularly enjoyable, students usually follow the rules so they can participate.

Extending the Use of Paired Repeated Reading

Because students enjoy working together and derive considerable pleasure and self confidence from hearing themselves read so well, they have asked to do it not just with the basal lesson but at other times of the day. The following are additional ways to use paired repeated reading:

- Paired repeated reading provides effective practice before students give written news or book reports, recite a poem, or read a favorite part of a book to an audience.
- To enhance writing skills and give students a sense of their audience, teachers have

had students repeatedly read sections to a partner to get a feel for the sound of their written language. Often students go back to revise their work after hearing their own or their partner's written language.

- Parents or friends are enthusiastic partners in repeated reading at home. Magazines or almost any type of material that interests the student can be used. This strategy gives interested parents a structured activity to do with their child. Their role is that of providing a word when asked and positive comments on improvement.

Few would argue the need for practice with meaningful natural text to learn and refine reading skill. In fact, most successful learners seem to seek the practice they need spontaneously. The challenge, however, is finding time for practice within the classroom day for students who are not automatically doing so.

Paired repeated reading is an effective and practical alternative. Student teams use typical classroom materials during follow-up to directed reading instruction. Both students and teachers find the strategy easy to learn and manage, and enjoyable. Most importantly, below average readers who use the strategy show considerable improvement in fluency, word recognition, and comprehension.

References

Allington, R.L. (1983, February). Fluency: The neglected reading goal. *The Reading Teacher, 36*, 556–561.

Allington, R.L. (1977, October). If they don't read much, how they ever gonna get good? *Journal of Reading, 21*, 57–61.

Allington, R.L. (1980, November/December). Poor readers don't get to read much in reading groups. *Language Arts, 57*, 872–876.

Anderson, R.C., Hiebert, E.H., Scott, J.H., & Wilkinson, I.A.B. (1985). *Becoming a nation of readers: The report of the Commission on Reading.* Washington, DC: National Institute of Education.

Blum, I.H., & Koskinen, P.S. (1982). *Enhancing fluency and comprehension through the use of repeated reading.* Paper presented at the College Reading Association conference, Philadelphia, PA.

Chomsky, C. (1976, March). After decoding: What? *Language Arts, 53*, 288–296, 314.

Downing, J. (1982, February). Reading—skill or skills? *The Reading Teacher, 35*, 534–537.

Durkin, D. (1978–1979). What classroom observations reveal about reading comprehension instruction. *Reading Research Quarterly, 14*(4), 481–523.

Gambrell, L.B. (1984). How much time do children spend reading during teacher-directed reading instruction? In J.A. Niles & L.A. Harris (Eds.), *Changing perspectives on research in reading/language processing and instruction* (33rd yearbook of the National Reading Conference, pp. 193–198). Rochester, NY: National Reading Conference.

Gambrell, L.B., Wilson, R.M., & Gantt, W.N. (1981, July/August). Classroom observations of task-attending behaviors of good and poor readers. *Journal of Educational Research, 74*, 400–404.

Herman, P.A. (1985, Fall). The effect of repeated readings on reading rate, speech pauses, and word recognition accuracy. *Reading Research Quarterly, 20*, 553–565.

Herman, P.A., Dewitz, P.A., & Stammer, J. (1980). *The development of syntactical chunking in non-fluent readers using the method of repeated reading.* Paper presented at the National Reading Conference, San Diego, CA.

Hiebert, E.H. (1983, Winter). An examination of ability grouping for reading instruction. *Reading Research Quarterly, 18*, 231–255.

Koskinen, P.S., & Blum, I.H. (1984). Repeated oral reading and the acquisition of fluency. In J.A. Niles & L.A. Harris (Eds.), *Changing perspectives on research in reading/language processing and instruction* (33rd yearbook of the National Reading Conference, pp. 183–187). Rochester, NY: National Reading Conference.

O'Shea, L.J., Sindelar, P.T., & O'Shea, D.J. (1985). The effects of repeated readings and attentional cues on reading fluency and comprehension. *Journal of Reading Behavior, 17*(2), 129–142.

Samuels, S.J. (1979, January). The method of repeated readings. *The Reading Teacher, 32*, 403–408.

Smith, F. (1982). *Understanding reading: A psycholinguistic analysis of reading and learning to read* (3rd ed.). New York: Holt, Rinehart and Winston.

Taylor, N.E., Wade, M.R., & Yekovich, F.R. (1985, Fall). The effects of text manipulation and multiple reading strategies on the reading performance of good and poor readers. *Reading Research Quarterly, 20*, 566–574.

Questions for Reflection

• The authors open the article by stressing the importance of providing opportunities to read. Do you feel you are giving students sufficient opportunities for reading practice with a variety of materials and purposes? For several days, track the amount of reading that takes place in your classroom. If you find that opportunities for authentic reading are limited, how can you use strategies like paired repeated reading to increase these opportunities?

• The authors state that working in pairs is "a privilege, not a right." Do you agree? Is this how you approach paired work in your classroom? How do you address classroom management challenges when students are working together in pairs or small groups?

Paired Reading: A Powerful Technique for Parent Use

Keith Topping

More and more parents are wanting to be closely involved in the education of their children. This desire has been reinforced in many countries by legislation which gives parents the *right* to be so involved.

Some teachers are very doubtful about these trends, resenting what they see as parental interference in school business, and are perhaps worried that misguided parents might harm their children's development. However, most teachers increasingly view parents as part of the solution rather than part of the problem, and are exploring ways in which teachers can use their professional expertise to guide parents into suitable methods for helping accelerate their children's educational progress. An ideal vehicle for such an exercise is Paired Reading.

Why a Particular Technique?

Research in the United Kingdom has shown that whether or not parents hear their children read at home is the major factor in children's reading progress, irrespective of socioeconomic status and a range of other variables (Hewison & Tizard, 1980). There is also evidence that even without training or guidance, most parents help their children with reading at home in a sensible way (Hannon, Jackson, & Weinberger, 1986). These authors found considerable similarities between parent and teacher strategies in helping children with reading.

However, parents were more likely to react to errors and showed less widespread concern for children's understanding. Parents tended to be a little more critical than teachers and less likely to provide a good model of reading, but nevertheless still provided a large proportion of difficult words for the children. Although parents did place more emphasis on phonic analysis than teachers, this was not to the extent that many teachers might have expected.

Subsequently, projects were operated in which parents in a disadvantaged area were encouraged to hear their children read, although not given any detailed guidance as to how to do this (Tizard, Schofield, & Hewison, 1982). This encouragement proved more effective in raising children's reading skills than providing extra professional reading tuition. Reading gains made by the parent-tutored children endured satisfactorily to long-term follow-up years later (Hewison, 1986).

Given the effectiveness of merely encouraging parents to hear their children read, attention then turned to increasing that effectiveness by developing packages for training parents in coherent techniques. It was hoped that these developments would not only increase the absolute effectiveness of parental input, but also promote parent involvement in a wider range of parents, including the disadvantaged, those of low literacy, and ethnic minority groups. In the United Kingdom, workers experimented with parent-tutored precision teaching, direct instruction packages, and a New Zealand technique knows as Pause Prompt and Praise. However, the most popular structured technique to date has undoubtedly been Paired Reading.

Reprinted from Topping, K. (1987). Paired Reading: A powerful technique for student use. *The Reading Teacher, 40*(7), 608–614.

Paired Reading Technique

A novel feature of the Paired Reading (PR) method is that *the child* chooses the reading material, irrespective of its level of difficulty. The technique allows for children to be supported through texts of high readability levels, with understanding supported by associated discussion and questioning. Most children quickly become quite skilled at choosing their own books.

During difficult text, the child is supported by the parent and child reading together—both read all the words out loud together, with the parent adjusting speed to achieve synchrony. The child must say every word correctly. Where the child makes an error, the adult merely repeats the word until the child reads it correctly. When encountering easier sections of text, the child makes some prearranged nonverbal signal to tell the parent to be quiet. This signal might be a knock, a nudge, or a squeeze. The child continues reading alone until an error is made, when the same correction procedure is applied, and the pair revert to reading together. There is much emphasis throughout on praise for correct reading, self correction, and signalling to read alone. The framework of the technique is outlined in the Figure.

Rationale for the Technique

Paired reading was designed to be inherently flexible, the intention being to maximise reading performance regardless of the child's existing method of attack on words through the use of generally applicable learning principles. The technique was intended to be standardised and simple to disseminate, and thus hopefully sufficiently robust to tolerate use over long periods by adults with limited supervision in competition with the hurly burly of the home environment.

The reading together aspect of PR was designed as participant modelling, in which the child received a model and continuous prompt for correct reading during his/her own attempt to read the words. The independent reading phase was to give the child practice in responses acquired during simultaneous reading. Praise was built in at specific points to reinforce important aspects of correct reading. Free choice of reading material was incorporated to increase interest and motivation and escape the inhibiting effects of simplified or special texts.

The technique specifies that children are not required to try any word for more than 5 seconds before being helped, and this was intended as a device for limiting child anxiety, widely acknowledged as a problem for failing readers.

Although PR was originally designed on behaviourist principles, it has since become clear that many psycholinguistic factors are at work in its success. The *reading together* aspect, coupled with the availability of virtually immediate support, frees many children from word by word decoding and enables them to read much more fluently with much greater consciousness of contextual cues. Word attack strategies may still be deployed by the child, but if they cannot be deployed rapidly and fluently within 5 seconds, support is immediately available.

Later workers have placed greater emphasis on embedding the Paired Reading technique in a context of language development, discussion and exploration at home of the meanings of unusual or unknown words. Even before this emphasis, however, the technique had already been found to improve children's reading *comprehension* more than their reading *accuracy* by virtue of making them more fluent, confident, and contextually oriented.

Thus the technique enables children to pursue their own interests and enthusiasms, leaves them more in control of what is going on, and eliminates failure. It is flexible and accommodates to the current level of interest, mood, degree of tiredness, difficulty of the book, and so on. The emphasis on continuity rather than stopping and starting gives children a more pleasurable experience which is added to by the frequent availability of praise and elimination of parental criticism. The incorporation of parent demonstration of good reading means that children can learn not only accurate oral reading, but also expressiveness, pacing, and attention to punctuation.

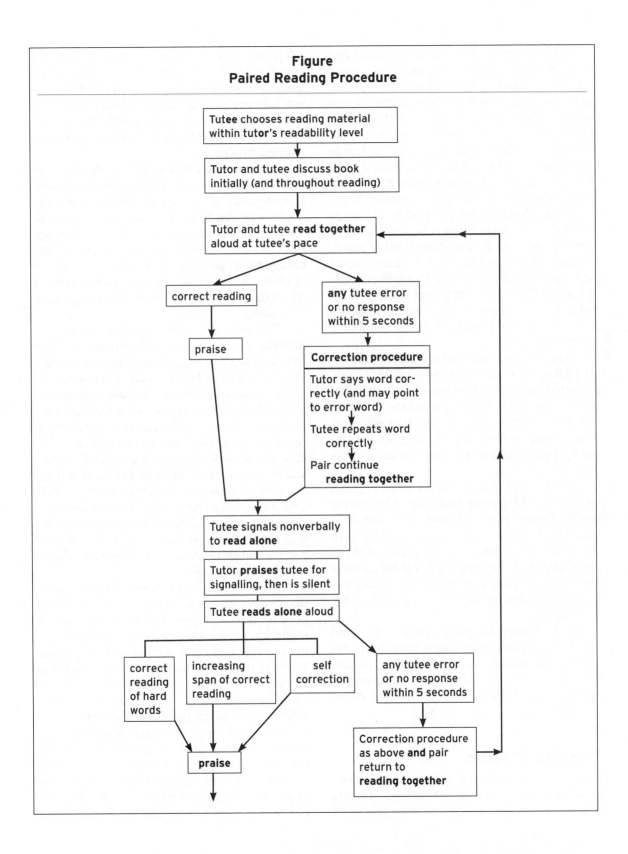

Figure
Paired Reading Procedure

Tutee chooses reading material within **tutor**'s readability level

Tutor and tutee discuss book initially (and throughout reading)

Tutor and tutee **read together** aloud at tutee's pace

correct reading

any tutee error or no response within 5 seconds

praise

Correction procedure

Tutor says word correctly (and may point to error word)

Tutee repeats word correctly

Pair continue **reading together**

Tutee signals nonverbally to **read alone**

Tutor **praises** tutee for signalling, then is silent

Tutee **reads alone** aloud

correct reading of hard words

increasing span of correct reading

self correction

any tutee error or no response within 5 seconds

Correction procedure as above **and** pair return to **reading together**

praise

Of course, involvement in a PR project also increases the amount of sheer practice at reading children get. And it gives children some peaceful private attention from their parents which may not otherwise be available. Perhaps most significantly, the technique gives parents a clear, coherent, straightforward, and enjoyable way of helping their children which is designed to be self reinforcing—so parents shouldn't get confused, worried, or bad tempered about reading.

These advantages are particularly relevant in parental involvement projects in disadvantaged or ethnic minority areas, where existing parental levels of literacy may be low. These parents may report that they can't read when they really only mean that their literacy level is low. The PR method can still be used, provided the readability of the material is controlled to be within the parents' competence.

Where the parents have no reading skills at all, siblings or members of the extended family can often be effectively trained to use the technique, while the parents supervise the work and give general praise and approval. However, such arrangements usually require some home visiting by a professional to ensure that all is going well.

Some schools have arranged to use PR via a sort of distance tutoring procedure, whereby the teacher reads a story onto audiotape; the child then takes the book and tape home to follow both simultaneously while receiving generalised parental approval. Commercially produced book and tape packages can also be used, but are less likely to be motivating and may include other distractions.

In the United Kingdom, the use of Paired Reading by parents from ethnic minorities who are English speaking has been excellent; in fact, the take-up from the Afro-Caribbean community has often been higher than from the White community.

Training Parents

Before proceeding to train parents, teachers must be fully conversant with the method. To this end, a video training pack has been produced (Topping, 1986b). Teachers should practise on cooperative children until they are firm on the technique, while bearing in mind that PR is essentially designed as a nonprofessional tutoring technique which may not necessarily be easy for teachers to acquire, given their own complex learning history.

It is essential that a first PR project is successful, and to this end it is desirable to start with a small group of children of a range of reading ability who can be closely supported and monitored. Care is needed to ensure that a wide range of books are available on easy access, for the children may get through a prodigious volume of books, and of course the factor of child choice may effectively render much of existing stock redundant.

The most economic form of training is probably to train parents and children together in one group meeting. Participants can view a knockabout role play or video of "How *Not* To Do It" as an amusing introduction. A brief lecture and written materials on the technique are unlikely to have any significant impact on parental practice; they need to be coupled with a demonstration of the procedure (either live or on video). Parents and children should then practise the technique and receive feedback and individual tuition as appropriate from teachers until the technique is mastered. Organisational details should be given and it may be desirable for parents and children to contract into the scheme more or less formally.

The children should choose books for practice in advance of the meeting, and at least one book must be well above the child's independent readability level, otherwise practice in *reading together* will not make sense to the parents. Times of meetings should be fixed to involve as many fathers as possible, since fathers do not always set good models of reading in the home, which may be particularly relevant for boys.

It is usual for parents and children to contract to an initial intensive period of using the technique. An arbitrary minimum involvement found useful in practice is 5 sessions per week of at least 5 minutes over 6 to 8 weeks. This initial commitment creates clear expectations for parents and ensures that the majority use the technique frequently enough both to become fluent and practised in it and also to see significant change in their children's reading ability, which should reinforce the parents into continuing using the technique in the longer term.

At the end of the initial period of commitment, the parents and children can be drawn back together to discuss their experiences and review where they would like to go from here. Many families wish to continue using the technique with the same frequency indefinitely, although some may choose to continue but less frequently, particularly if the weather is improving and hours of daylight extending. A few parents wish to stop altogether or use a different technique (further details of parental continuation choices are reported in Topping, 1986a).

During the intensive phase of the project, monitoring of parent–child practice is highly desirable. Many schools use a simple home–school diary record system, with the family recording books read and positive comments on child progress, which are reviewed weekly by the co-ordinating teacher. Observing children choosing books in school and questioning them about their Paired Reading at home can provide revealing insights. Many schools arrange teacher–parent meetings in school during the project, which can be either individual or group, to review progress and ensure the technique has not drifted.

When parents are hard to reach or have other difficulties, home visits by the coordinating or class teacher often prove extremely valuable. Experience shows that these are universally welcomed by parents and children alike, and it is very rare for them to be seen as an intrusion even in the most disadvantaged neighbourhoods.

It is desirable to build some form of evaluation into the project, in order to be able to feed back the results to the parents and children to enhance their motivation to continue. There may also be benefits in having tangible evaluation information to hand for convincing sceptical colleagues. Evaluation methodology could include norm referenced or criterion referenced reading tests on a before and after basis. If baseline and follow-up information can be collected, so much the better.

Many teachers also like to test a control or comparison group. Other more qualitative assessments could be used, involving informal reading inventories, cloze tests, forms of miscue or error analysis, and so on. The verbal observations of participating parents, children, and class teachers can be noted or audiorecorded, and many schools also use a simple form of feedback questionnaire or checklist.

It is always worthwhile to ensure that your first project is very methodically organised, since your credibility in the community will stand or fall by its success. A successful first project may result in the school being overwhelmed with requests for similar training by many other parents.

Evaluation Research

Education has suffered from more than its fair share of passing fashions over the years. Many teachers are sensibly doubtful about the supposed virtues of new methods, until they have been proven to be effective. While Paired Reading does not pretend to be any sort of panacea, there is now a great deal of research evidence on the positive impact of the method on children's reading skills.

Normal improvements in reading skills can be defined as an increase in reading age on reading tests exactly proportionate to the passage of time. Evaluation studies show that children involved in Paired Reading on average make 3 times normal progress in reading accuracy and 5 times normal progress in reading comprehension. At the time of writing, over 100 studies had been listed in a bibliography on the subject (Topping, 1986b), so a metaanalysis of the results of projects for very various groups of children is possible.

Paired Reading has been demonstrated to be effective with children of all levels of assumed ability and potential, ranging from children in special schools for slow learners through to children who are above average in intelligence or reading skill. Children aged between 6 and

13 years have participated successfully, and the technique has now been extended into the field of adult literacy.

Socioeconomic status has not been found to correlate with the success of projects, and even in disadvantaged areas parental involvement has been sustained over long periods. (For convenient means of accessing a number of the more significant of the studies, see Topping and Wolfendale, 1985.) A summary of evaluation results on well over 1,000 children from one local education authority is available (in Topping, 1986a).

Of course, crude reading tests by no means tell the whole story. The subjective perceptions of the parents and children involved in projects are also very important, particularly with respect to understanding PR's affective outcomes. In data from a random sample of 345 parental feedback questionnaires at least two thirds of the children were reported by their parents to be reading more, more widely, and with more enthusiasm, interest, and enjoyment, and with more understanding and confidence. Also, 71% were said to be more accurate readers and 72% more fluent. Greater expressiveness was shown by 55% (Topping, 1986a).

Data from a random sample of 202 feedback questionnaires completed by participating children were even more encouraging. Learning the technique was found easy by 85% of the children, and 77% reported liking doing it; 88% said they now liked all reading better, and 94% felt they were now more competent readers.

Keeping Parents Involved

There are now a number of well elaborated strategies for involving parents in the reading development of their children. Paired Reading seems deceptively simple and many of its components are certainly not new. However, a substantial body of research evidence suggests that this technique constitutes a simple, coherent, durable, and easily deliverable package for parents and other nonprofessionals. The technique should be included in the repertoire of all teachers interested in parental involvement.

References

Hannon, P., Jackson, A., & Weinberger, J. (1986, March). Parents' and teachers' strategies in hearing young children read. *Research Papers in Education, 1,* 6–25.

Hewison, J. (1986, December). *Haringey revisited: Three years after a parental involvement in reading project.* Paper presented at the London Conference of the British Psychological Association, London, England.

Hewison, J., & Tizard, J. (1980, November). Parental involvement and reading attainment. *British Journal of Educational Psychology, 50,* 209–215.

Tizard, J., Schofield, B.N., & Hewison, J. (1982, February). Collaboration between teachers and parents in assisting children's reading. *British Journal of Educational Psychology, 52,* 1–15.

Topping, K.J. (1986a, October–December). Effective service delivery: Training parents as reading tutors. *School Psychology International, 7,* 231–236.

Topping, K.J. (1986b). *Paired Reading training pack* (2nd ed.). Huddersfield, England: Kirklees Psychological Service.

Topping, K.J., & Wolfendale, S. (Eds.). (1985). *Parental involvement in children's reading.* London: Croom Helm; New York: Nichols.

Questions for Reflection

• In a note to this article's original publication in a 1987 issue of *The Reading Teacher*, the journal editor points out the differences and similarities between paired reading described here (involving parents) and in an earlier article by Koskinen and Blum (involving pairs of children). Both articles are included in this volume. The journal editor suggests that "Those who like cooperative teaching methods will enjoy comparing the two articles." What are your thoughts when you make that comparison yourself?

• The author stresses the importance of success with your first home–school paired reading project. How can you work with colleagues to share the responsibility for ensuring this success? Can you enlist the support of your school administrators? How can you plan for follow-up projects, particularly if, as the author suggests may happen, the school is "overwhelmed with requests" to expand your successful PR program?

• Paired reading is reported here as a parental involvement project, but it is also described as "inherently flexible." How might you adapt paired reading for in-school use? Who can you enlist to take on the tutor role? What about older students or even classmates more able at reading? Do you have access to adult volunteers who could participate? What adaptations to organization might be needed?

The Akron Paired Reading Project

Timothy V. Rasinski and Anthony D. Fredericks

Imagine what might happen if parents whose children were experiencing difficulty in reading spent at least 5 minutes every day reading with their youngsters. Children's reading would certainly improve. Children would learn that reading is important at home as well as at school. And they would receive the undivided attention and affection of their mom or dad for a few minutes every day. For their part, parents would learn about their children's reading difficulties and develop some sensitivity to the teacher's job. For most teachers this would be a dream come true. In the Akron Public Schools it's beginning to happen—now.

After reading and discussing the paired reading program described in a recent article of *The Reading Teacher* (Topping, 1987), Gloria Dallinga, Program Manager of Chapter 1 [now Title I] Reading for Ohio's Akron Public Schools, decided to try paired reading with the students and parents in the Chapter 1 classes. Gloria and several of the Chapter 1 teachers saw the paired reading program as a positive way to satisfy the Chapter 1 mandate for training parents to participate actively in their children's learning.

Developed in England, paired reading allows parents to provide structured practice in contextual reading for their children. Research suggests that poor readers lack opportunities to practice reading and that they are often placed in environments that discourage reading (Stanovich, 1986). In paired reading, parents read along with their children in a book of their child's choosing. Parents adjust their oral participation according to the difficulty that the child experiences. In parts of the text where the child reads with fluency the parent switches to silent reading and allows the child to read orally by him or herself.

Besides getting much needed reading practice, the children have a model of a fluent reader—the parent—and they experience reading in a warm, encouraging environment. Research has demonstrated that children engaging in paired reading for only 5 to 15 minutes a day make significant gains in fluency and comprehension.

Dallinga and a core group of four Chapter 1 reading teachers decided that paired reading was worth a try for the 1989–90 school year in Akron Public Schools. During the summer preceding the school year, the core committee made preparations for introducing paired reading in the fall to fellow Chapter 1 teachers and parents. Gloria wrote to England to obtain more information from Keith Topping, an expert in paired reading. Sue Gump and Jackie Orosz, Chapter 1 reading teachers at Barrett School, planned inservice training on paired reading for teachers and parents and also developed a demonstration of paired reading with Jackie acting as the child and Sue as the parent. Two other teachers on the core committee developed printed packets that included instructions, record sheets, contracts, and other informational material on paired reading.

At the August inservice training all the Chapter 1 reading teachers were introduced to paired reading. All parents whose children were in the Chapter 1 reading program would be asked to participate in paired reading with their children for at least 5 minutes per day. Chapter 1 teachers were given the responsibility for training the parents of their own Chapter 1 students. Gloria and the other members of the

Reprinted from Rasinski, T.V., & Fredericks, A.D. (1991). The Akron paired reading project (Working With Parents). *The Reading Teacher*, 44(7), 514–515.

core committee were available to help teachers in parental training.

Mary Lu Ramsey, a Chapter 1 reading teacher at Reidinger Middle School and St. Mary's Elementary School, found it easy to get parents involved. She held six separate training sessions for her students' parents. When she emphasized to parents that paired reading is easy to learn and do, works with all ages of children using all kinds of texts from books to newspapers, takes only a few minutes each day, and has been proven to work, parents were eager to begin. In fact, Mary Lu found that many parents attending the training sessions didn't have children in the Chapter 1 program. They had heard about paired reading at parent–teacher meetings and through the school grapevine.

All of the Akron Public Schools had excellent levels of parent participation. In some schools teachers made home visits to train parents who couldn't attend the training sessions held in the school. Seven of 43 schools in the school district trained 100% of the parents of Chapter 1 students in their respective schools. Overall, 400 parents were trained and agreed to try paired reading with their children. Teachers also held follow-up meetings to answer parents' questions and to maintain parents' paired reading skills. After the training, parents and their children signed contracts in which they agreed to engage in paired reading for 5 minutes each evening for 3 months.

To make paired reading special, parents were encouraged to find a comfortable, quiet place in which to read. Only the parent and child are together during paired reading. During the program, parents and children read one book chosen by the child each week. Children choose books at a suitable reading level that appeal to them from their schools and libraries.

Jean McNulty, another Chapter 1 teacher, used decorated boxes to separate books by grade levels. All second grade books, for example, were kept in a box decorated with animals. Fourth grade books could be found in the spaceship box. These boxes made it easy for students to choose books that were appropriate to their reading level.

Friday was Paired Reading Day at many schools; on Friday children returned the books they read with their parents during the week and chose new ones. At school the children were also given the opportunity to read portions of the books they had read at home, gaining the praise of their teacher and classmates.

Some children's interest in paired reading waned after a few weeks. To keep students and parents motivated, Jackie and Sue instituted a token economy. Children who read at least 35 minutes with their parents during the previous week (documented by a parent on a signed record sheet) were given 10 dollars in play money that could be exchanged later for books and other prizes.

After 3 months of paired reading, Sue and Jackie held a breakfast meeting to celebrate the parents' and students' participation. Although they felt the program had had a powerful, positive effect on many of their students' reading, Sue and Jackie were interested in the reactions of the parents. When the two teachers solicited written comments they found parents overwhelmingly positive in their evaluation of paired reading. Many of the responses demonstrated that paired reading not only improved reading performance, it also helped to improve children's desire to read and strengthened the bond of affection between parents and children.

Of the 25 parents who attended the Barrett School breakfast, all said that they wanted to continue paired reading with their children. Moreover, half of the parents asked for a review training session.

One mother of a first-grader wrote, "Paired reading has really helped Paul—he loves to read now." Another mother wrote, "Reading with Chris has improved his reading and also is bringing Chris and me closer." Another parent of a first grader said she could "see L'Tanya's improvement in the 3 months that we have been using the paired reading system." And a mother who was skeptical at first admitted that there was something good about paired reading: "At first, I thought this was silly and that it couldn't make much difference in Katie's reading. Then I saw the improvement myself. We both had fun together, and she was reading. I now believe in the program and really enjoy it."

Students also reacted positively to paired reading. Mary Lu Ramsey's sixth-grade students told her that they liked the special time they had with their parents.

Reading is perceived by many parents as too complicated for them to teach. And many ill-conceived attempts by parents to help their children end up in frustration and disappointment. Paired reading offers the possibility of making parental involvement in reading easy, effective, and enjoyable.

The teachers also reflected positively on paired reading. Jackie, who is a 17-year veteran of Chapter 1 reading programs, stated, "Paired reading and Reading Recovery are the best things to have happened in the remedial reading programs." Both Jackie and Sue noted that their Chapter 1 students who participated in paired reading became more fluent readers. They both observed less word-by-word reading and noted that sight word recognition and vocabulary also improved. Finally Jackie and Sue observed that students were willing to read, enjoyed reading more, and were less likely to act out during reading time.

Chapter 1 teachers in Akron plan to continue developing, expanding, and improving their paired reading program. Although a training/ introductory tape was sent from England, plans for the coming year include developing their own video demonstration using children and parents from the local community doing paired reading.

Many teachers and parents would like more training in paired reading. Topics that might be addressed in further training include finding time for paired reading, choosing the right books, developing nonverbal ways for the child to signal the parent that he/she would like to read alone, including other family members in paired reading, and extending paired reading over the summer months.

We have little doubt that the Chapter 1 reading staff in the Akron Public Schools will continue to make paired reading meet the needs and concerns of their students. When teachers and parents are informed about ways of helping children learn to read and are empowered to set their ideas in motion, making modifications as they see fit, wonderful things, like paired reading, can and do happen.

References

Stanovich, K.E. (1986). Matthew effects in reading: Some consequences of individual differences in the acquisition of literacy. *Reading Research Quarterly, 21,* 360–406.

Topping, K. (1987). Paired reading: A powerful technique for parent use. *The Reading Teacher, 40,* 608–614.

Questions for Reflection

• Do you think that involving parents in paired reading would work in your school or district? What do you know about your students' home environments that would influence the way you might approach working with parents in such a program? For example, do you have English-language learners in your class whose parents may have limited English fluency? How might you adjust your approach to take into account the particular home situations of your students?

• The article focuses on paired reading as implemented with students in a compensatory education program. Do you think the approach could be successfully implemented with students in mainstream classes? In gifted/talented programs? What modifications would you make?

An Experimental Approach
to the Impress Method
of Teaching Reading

Paul M. Hollingsworth

The teacher of reading who is constantly searching for a better, more efficient means of developing reading skills—especially teachers who are working with children who are underachievers or reluctant to use reading skills—should become aware of the impress method (often called the neurological impress reading method).

The impress method is a reading process in which the child and teacher read aloud simultaneously. The book is held jointly, and the teacher, who is placed slightly behind the pupil, directs her/his voice into the ear of the child. Child and teacher read aloud simultaneously. The pupil slides his/her finger along the lines, following the words as they are spoken. In this way the child's visual, aural, oral, and tactile senses are involved in the reading process.

The goal of the impress method is to read as many pages of material as time permits without causing physical discomfort. During the impress reading period, no attention is called to the pictures accompanying the reading materials nor does the teacher attempt to teach sounds of words or word recognition skills. The child is not asked comprehension questions after the reading session. The teacher should, though, remark positively on the success of the child, calling attention to the fluency of his/her reading.

The impress method is easy to use but it is time-consuming, especially if several pupils in the classroom need this type of approach. Even if a teacher had the time to read with the pupils, the physical discomfort and fatigue of the teacher's voice would be another limiting factor.

These two limiting factors can be overcome by using the EFI Multi-Channel Wireless Language System. With this system, each child hears a tape recording and her/his own voice simultaneously through a headset. The wireless system eliminates the need for the teacher to read with each child and allows the teacher to monitor 10 children at the same time.

A study of the wireless system for the impress method with fourth grade normal readers (Hollingsworth, 1970) showed no significant differences in reading achievement between eight children who used the wireless and matched controls who did not. However, it was surmised that the technique might be more effective with remedial readers who were more in need of the support from several sense modalities. Therefore a second investigation was planned. Significant changes included: (1) only remedial readers participated, and (2) the number of sessions using the wireless doubled, from 30 to 62.

The children who participated in this new study were fourth, fifth, and sixth grade remedial reading pupils from the Washoe County School District, Nevada. Twenty children ranging in IQ from 79 to 128 according to the Peabody Picture Vocabulary Test were randomly assigned to

Reprinted from Hollingsworth, P.M. (1978). An experimental approach to the impress method of teaching reading. *The Reading Teacher, 31*(6), 624–626.

43

either an experimental or control group. Each group had a total of ten pupils. All children in both groups were given the Gates–MacGinitie Reading Test, Survey D, Form 1, and the Peabody Picture Vocabulary Test, Form A, in February 1977. Form 2 of the Gates–MacGinitie was used as a posttest in May.

Tapes were used for the EFI Multi-Channel Wireless Language System, using various stories of interest for fourth, fifth, and sixth grade pupils. Prerecorded tapes were made for each grade level from first to sixth grade. To add variety to the taped materials, both female and male voices were used. Each tape was approximately 12 to 15 minutes long.

Each child in the experimental group read a story each day during the spring semester. One third of the sessions, the children read stories one grade level below their reading achievement level as determined by the Gates–MacGinitie Reading Test; one third of the sessions, the pupils read stories at their reading level; and the final third of the sessions, the stories were one grade level above.

While the stories were being broadcast, the children read aloud into their own mikes, which were attached to their individual headsets. In this arrangement the children could hear their own voices on the tape along with the prerecorded voice. The teacher went from child to child and plugged her/his headset into the child's individual receiving set to determine if the child was reading with the taped voice and if the pupil's finger was under the words read. The teacher could monitor 10 children quite successfully in this manner.

The children in the control group continued in the regular program provided in their classroom by the classroom teacher. The control group had no more nor less reading time than the experimental group.

After 62 daily sessions of approximately 15 minutes each (a total of 15½ hours), the posttest was administered to both groups. The data from the tests were analyzed statistically by using the analysis of covariance, with the level of confidence set at 5%. The intelligence test score of each child from the Peabody test and the comprehension subtest score from the Gates–MacGinitie, Form 1, were used as the covariates.

A test of significance was made of the null hypothesis that pupils who received the impress treatment do not differ in reading comprehension achievement from those pupils who had not received the impress treatment. The analysis of covariance indicated $F(1, 16) = 6.44$, $p < .05$.

There was a signficant difference found between the two groups in reading comprehension as measured by the Gates–MacGinitie, Form 2 posttest. When pre- and posttest mean scores in comprehension were compared, it was seen that the experimental group made one year's growth during the semester. The control group mean score changes were only .04 of a year's growth during this same time period.

The impress method for teaching reading in this small study of remedial reading children in the upper elementary grades was effective when using the EFI Multi-Channel Wireless Language System. Not only did the children in the experimental group raise their reading comprehension scores, but they seemed to enjoy the whole procedure as observed by their remarks and eagerness to use the EFI Multi-Channel Wireless Language System each day.

Reference

Hollingsworth, P.M. (1970). An experiment with the impress method of teaching reading. *The Reading Teacher*, *24*(2), 112–114, 187.

Questions for Reflection

• This article was published in 1978, considerably before the widespread availability of computers in classrooms and schools. How might you use today's technology to facilitate implementation of the impress method of assisted reading? What benefits might this technology offer over the tools that the author describes?

• The author indicates that the tapes used contained "stories of interest" to fourth- through sixth-grade students, and that the recordings used male and female voices for variety. How would you go about selecting stories to record for use in assisted reading? How would you vary readers to ensure diversity?

• The author's research focused on students in the upper elementary grades, particularly those who were experiencing difficulty with reading. Do you think the impress method might benefit younger students? Older students? Students at a range of ability levels?

Teaching Reading With Talking Books

Marie Carbo

If you have agonized with students who struggle and stumble as they read, expending their energies merely deciphering words, barely comprehending, this article is for you. You may find the three "talking book" reading methods described here useful in helping these students become more fluent readers with better comprehension.

For three years I have used talking books (specially tape recorded books) to teach reading to children with severe learning handicaps, including the learning disabled, educable retarded, emotionally disturbed, and severely speech impaired. All of the students have made substantial gains in comprehension, word recognition, and word meaning. Moreover, after the talking book experience, some fo the children appear to have understood intuitively and applied phonics rules without formal phonics instruction. Talking books seem to serve as a readiness activity for phonics instruction by enabling students to develop a basic sight vocabulary from which phonics rules may be drawn.

Teaching reading with talking books appears to be particularly effective with youngsters who have memory problems and/or difficulty learning to read through the phonics approach, and for older students who, after repeated failure, have been turned off to reading. Talking books enable older students with some reading skills to read material on their language comprehension level, and help them to integrate the rate, rhythm, and nature flow of language necessary for good comprehension. In addition, with talking books, students make fewer reading errors and the possibility of forming incorrect reading patterns is diminished. From the very beginning, talking books provide youngsters with the correct reading model to imitate. And, as a result, the success which youngsters experience with the talking book method builds their self-confidence and makes them more willing to invest further effort in learning to read.

Searching for a Special Method

The talking book reading methods were initially designed for eight learning disabled students of average intelligence, in grades two to six, who had memory problems, attention difficulties, and most importantly, auditory perception deficiencies. They could not easily discriminate between the sounds represented by letters (much as a tone-deaf person cannot discriminate between musical notes), nor could they easily blend sounds to form words. Furthermore, their attention and memory problems made it difficult for them to remember whole words. Therefore, their sight vocabulary was minimal. When these youngsters, who were reading two to four years below grade level, tried to read a page of print, they did not see words which formed sentences and paragraphs. Instead, they saw a page with hundreds of individual letters which had to be deciphered, remembered, and then blended in the correct sequence to form words—an impossible task for them.

It was regrettable that many of these children had been exposed to intensive phonics instruction early in their schooling. Lerner (1971) has cautioned against the continuous use of a phonics approach with a youngster who has a serious deficit in the auditory modality because it may lead to "frustration, failure and a dislike

Reprinted from Carbo, M. (1978). Teaching reading with talking books. *The Reading Teacher, 32*(3), 267–273.

of reading and the teacher." Evidently, at some critical point in the learning process, many of these learning disabled students had been taught to read through their weakest modality. It was no wonder that they perceived the reading process as a series of endless, unrelated obstacles to be surmounted. They were, therefore, poor readers in the most basic sense; they did not understand that the fundamental purpose of reading is thought communication.

I sought a special reading method for these learning disabled students which would utilize their individual learning styles, as recommended by Dunn and Dunn (1975). The method, I concluded, would have to possess these characteristics: (1) multisensory, to compensate for their perception deficits; (2) high interest, to hold their attention; (3) in context, to increase their comprehension; (4) highly structured with instant feedback, to promote steady growth and feelings of security; and (5) fail-safe, to improve their self-concept. In addition, sufficient repetition, which could be controlled by the student, would be needed to overcome memory deficiencies.

I knew that research had demonstrated that the process of reading aloud to children produced growth in vocabulary, word knowledge, and visual decoding (Baily, 1970; Chomsky, 1972; Cohen, 1968). Moreover, Heckelman (1969) had used his "neurological impress method" to improve reading skills. [In Heckelman's method an instructor is positioned behind the student. The student holds the book to be read, while the instructor traces her/his fingers below the words, reading the words aloud with the student. The neurological impress method did eliminate the need to rely on the phonic skills of students; printed words would not have to be deciphered. Instead, students could see and hear the words within the context of a story.]

Heckelman's method, however, might not provide sufficient repetition, and many of the learning disabled students might be embarrassed if they had to learn in the presence of an instructor. Tape recorded books seemed to be the answer, since a student could read along with the voice of a recorded instructor and could in this way learn the passage in private. Furthermore, students would be assured of success with talking books since they would read aloud only after a tape recording had provided sufficient repetition to enable learning to take place.

As a beginning step, I observed how the eight students used commercially recorded books. Although Carol Chomsky (1976) would later report reading gains using commercially recorded books with average third graders, these learning disabled students could not keep their places in the story and, therefore, had no way of associating what they heard with the printed words on the page. Special recording procedures had to be developed in order to transform tape recorded books into reading lessons, and to allow these handicapped students to associate the printed words with the words spoken on the tape recording. Consequently, I devised three recording techniques which synchronized for the student the printed words with the tape recorded words, and the "talking book" method was born.

Recording Techniques

1. *Cueing the listener.* I numbered the book pages consecutively (if they were not already numbered) and cued the youngster for whom I was recording by stating the page number before reading the page. Next, I paused long enough to allow the listener to turn to the correct page, look at the pictures, and find the first line of print.

2. *Phrase reading.* I recorded the material with particular emphasis on clarity, expression, and logical phrasing. The latter seemed to help the students to assimilate natural word groupings and lessen their tendency to read word-by-word.

3. *Tactual reinforcement.* To help the children keep pace with the taped reading and focus better on the task, I instructed them to move their finger under the words as they heard them. Part of a talking book recording is reproduced below. Notice that

the page cues are consistently reduced until only the page number is stated.

Book Number Eight

The Little King, the Little Queen and the Little Monster

Open the book to page one. [long pause]

Move your finger under the words as you hear them.

Page one. [pause]

There was/ a little boy/

who had always/ wished to be king.

Turn to page three. [pause]

So that night/ the Good Fairy came/

and asked,/ "What is your wish?"/

And the little boy/ told her,/

"I wish/ to be a king."

Page five. [pause]

The Good Fairy/ granted the

little boy's wish./

Six. [pause]

Sound effects were not used on any of the recordings, in order to reduce the possibility of auditory distractions and, thereby, to increase the student's focus on the spoken and printed words.

Recording Entire Books

This method helped the students associate printed language with spoken language, train their eyes to move from left to right, improve their reading rate and rhythm, and experience the enjoyment of understanding and discussing books. The eight learning disabled students learned through this method for three months, and, on an achievement test, made the following gains in word recognition: time lapse—3 months; average gain—3 months; highest gain—5 months; lowest gain—2 months. Of course these are rough measures, but they indicate definite improvement in student who previously had shown severely below average gains on similar tests.

I recorded 30 paperback books ranging in reading level from second to fifth grade. Each book was numbered and then recorded on one side of a tape cassette which had the corresponding number. The eight students were permitted to select freely from among the books.

Most of the students were able to follow the recording visually (seeing the words), aurally (hearing the words), and tactually (tracing the words with their fingers). All of the children enjoyed the recorded books and discussed them with interest and good comprehension after working with the tapes.

For many of the students this was a major breakthrough. They began to understand that reading can be stimulating and enjoyable—perhaps a skill worthy of effort. Moreover, some of the youngsters were even able to read a book without the accompanying tape after listening to it several times. This was a feat they had never before accomplished and one that made them proud.

This first method can be used by both classroom teachers and specialists. It increases reading enjoyment and comprehension, helps youngster associate printed language with spoken language, and lets them experience the enjoyment of reading and understanding an entire book.

Recording Parts of Books

The objectives of the second talking book method were identical to the first, with this important addition: to enable students to read material on their language comprehension level with correct pacing, phrasing, voice inflection, and rate, regardless of their low reading ability.

The real potential of the talking book method became more evident when individual tape recordings were made for the eight learning disabled students. In online three months, the gains in word recognition were phenomenal, especially when compared to past performance. What is more, the highest gains were made by sixth graders who, for the first time, were able to read material on or near their grade level even though their actual reading level was three and four years below grade level. Note the extraordinary gains: time lapse—3 months; average gain—8 months; highest gain—15 months; lowest gain—4 months.

On a daily basis, I made tape recordings of parts of books for each student. The choice of books varied according to the age and reading level of the child. Children who were beginning to read were assigned basal readers with a controlled vocabulary, while the students in grades four through six were permitted to select books closer to their language comprehension level rather than their reading level.

When tape-recording for a student, both my reading rate and phrase length depended upon the reading ability of the potential listener. For example, if an upper grader with poor reading skills chose a difficult book, I recorded the selection using short word groups (two to four words), at a slower than usual rate, and in small quantities (as little as one paragraph). The length of the recorded passage (from one paragraph to about five pages) was dependent upon the amount of material that the potential listener could digest in one sitting and then read back to me with relative ease, as observed on several trials. As the youngster's reading improved, I gradually quickened my recording pace, lengthened the phrases, and increased the quantity. If a student chose a book below his/her reading level (which was unusual), then I recorded the material at a normal rate, in longer phrases, and in larger quantities. To summarize, when recording for a child, I considered: (1) the extent of his/her interest in the book; (2) the maximum phrase length he/she could assimilate; (3) the maximum reading rate at which he/she could follow; and (4) the amount of material he/she could digest in one sitting.

Every day the students received their individual tape recording and book. The students usually chose to listen to their tape three or four times. When a child read a passage back to me, I helped to focus her/his attention on phrases instead of individual words by visibly surrounding each phrase with my thumb and index finger to form a semicircle above the phrase to be read. This visual phrasing reinforced the auditory phrasing on the recording and helped to lessen reversals and word-by-word readings.

After the students listened to their individually recorded books, they were able to read the material back to me. It was a delight to hear the change in their oral reading. Instead of their previous slow, hesitant, labored reading, they now read with enthusiasm and expression, appropriately altering their voice and pacing to suit the mood of the passage. They understood, enjoyed, and could read their books.

The greatest gain in word recognition (15 months) was made by Tommy, a sixth grade boy reading on a 2.2 level. Prior to working with the tapes, he had faltered and stumbled over second grade words while his body actually shook with fear and discomfort. Understandably, he hated to read. Because a beloved teacher had once read *Charlotte's Web* to him, he asked me to record his favorite chapter from this book. I recorded one paragraph on each cassette side so that Tommy could choose to read either one or two paragraphs daily. The first time that he listened to a recording (five times) and then read the passage silently to himself (twice), he was able to read the passage to me perfectly, with excellent expression and without fear. After this momentous event, Tommy worked hard. At last he knew he was capable of learning to read and was willing to give it all he could. The result was a 15 month gain in word recognition at the end of only three months. Every learning disabled child in the program experienced immediate success with her/his individually recorded books.

This second method can also be used by both classroom teachers and specialists. Since individual tape recordings are time-consuming to make for large numbers of students, teachers might want to assemble a group of volunteers and train them in the recording techniques described here. Pair each volunteer with one student so the volunteer assumes recording responsibility for that student. Assign material to be recorded to each volunteer on a regular basis.

Programming Tape Recorded Books

The third reading method combined strategies used in both the first and second methods. In order to avoid having to erase each student's tape each night to record new material, I decided to program talking books. Each book would be sequenced, with small gradations of difficulty between successive books, and then recorded in small segments, since this strategy had been so successful in the second method. Programming allowed for the accumulation of permanent book recordings with supplementary materials such as activity cards, games, audio cards, and reading skills exercises. Furthermore, since individual tape recordings no longer had to be made, greater numbers of students could participate, and new entrants could be diagnosed and easily and accurately assigned appropriate talking book materials. After three months, the eight students made excellent gains in word recognition, although the gains were not as large as they had been with the personalized tape recordings: time lapse—3 months; average gain—6 months; highest gain—9 months; lowest gain—3 months.

I selected and sequenced in order of difficulty 100 high-interest paperback books (ranging from first to fifth grade). I recorded each book in small segments so that every child in the program could successfully complete one tape recording at a sitting. I noted on a chart the number of the cassette side and the pages recorded on it. A short book might require only two tape sides, a longer book as many as ten. This crucial recording of small amounts would later eliminate virtually all feelings of frustration or failure on the part of the students. Every child would be capable of completing at least one tape cassette per day, or approximately one to three books per week.

Record keeping was accurate and minimal. I duplicated a chart of the books and had only to color in the box on the chart which corresponded to the book and tape side read by the youngster, indicate the date, and then make notations about the student's reading progress. Individual programs were written for the students on a weekly basis, and even the most severely disabled students had no difficulty following them, or locating and returning materials. "Book 15(3)" written on a child's program simply meant "book number 15, tape side three."

Efficient System

This third method helped the youngsters improve their reading skills substantially and evolved into an efficient and smooth-running system. As new youngsters entered the program, they could be tested and immediately assigned appropriate materials. The permanently recorded materials and high degree of organization made it possible to train volunteers to work with the children. Not only was one-to-one instruction provided for each youngster through the tape readings, but, in addition, volunteers worked individually with the students on the games, skills lessons, and activities which were devised to accompany the recorded books.

Programmed talking books can be used by a classroom teacher but are most suitable for use by a specialist working with large numbers of students. This method allows the specialist to program materials that are ideal for his/her students and to develop a smooth, workable, stable program in which children can make steady, substantial reading progress.

Each of the talking book reading methods proved to be successful with the eight learning disabled students described in this article and with other youngsters with severe learning handicaps. Repeatedly in the past three years I have seen nonreaders and poor readers transformed into enthusiastic learners after their first experience with talking books.

A supplementary programmed and tape recorded word study skills program is used after the youngsters have developed both a sight vocabulary and security in and affection for books. It is important to note that none of the three talking book strategies requires phonic skills. They do provide high-interest, in-context material with adequate repetition, and allow the student to determine when he/she is ready to perform. With talking books, students can experience immediate success. I have found that the talking book method has what Roswell and Natchez (1964) term a "psychotherapeutic" effect on the personalities of the students. Not only have all the youngsters made excellent gains in reading compared to previous performance, but they have become more interested in reading, more willing to try, and more helpful toward one another.

References

Baily, G. (1970). *The use of a library resource program for improvement of language abilities of disadvantaged first grade pupils of an urban community.* Doctoral dissertation, Boston College, Chestnut Hill, MA.

Chomsky, C. (1972). Stages in language development and reading exposure. *Harvard Educational Review, 42,* 1–33.

Chomsky, C. (1976). After decoding: What? *Language Arts, 53,* 288–296.

Cohen, D. (1968). Effect of literature on vocabulary and reading. *Elementary English, 45,* 209–213.

Dunn, R., & Dunn, K. (1975). *Educator's self-teaching guide to individualized instructional programs.* West Nyack, NY: Parker.

Heckelman, R.G. (1969). A neurological impress method of reading instruction. *Academic Therapy, 44,* 277–282.

Lerner, J. (1971). *Children with learning disabilities.* Boston, MA: Houghton Mifflin.

Roswell, F., & Natchez, G. (1964). *Reading disability: Diagnosis and treatment.* New York: Basic Books.

Questions for Reflection

• The author describes her work with eight learning-disabled children. Do you think the talking book method she outlines would benefit children performing at or above grade level? Or children performing below grade level who are not learning disabled? How might the three modifications the author presents be further modified for use with children at different ability levels?

• Because preparation of the talking book materials and implementation of the instructional method are time consuming, the author recommends enlisting volunteers to assist. In his introduction to this collection, Timothy Rasinski suggests that students themselves might make recordings for their peers. In what other ways could you adjust the approach to make it more manageable in your classroom? For example, what technology is now available that might be used effectively? Could you use peers or older students to assist the children in your class?

• Consider this article together with the preceding piece by Paul Hollingsworth. What do they tell you about effective instructional approaches involving oral reading?

"I Never Thought I Could Be a Star": A Readers Theatre Ticket to Fluency

Miriam Martinez, Nancy L. Roser, and Susan Strecker

Five second graders make their way, scripts in hand, to the front of the classroom. They giggle with anticipation as they turn their backs to the audience. "Ladies and gentlemen," their teacher announces, "the Readers Theatre of Room 313 proudly presents an adaptation of Edward Marshall's *Fox in Love!*" Five performers turn on cue, and Juanita begins: "Well, wait until the girls hear about this!" She reads saucily, and the narrator's words follow to explain that Raisin (played by Juanita) has just seen her boyfriend, Fox, with another girl. The second-grade audience frowns disapprovingly; the performance promises to be yet another success for the repertory group. As always, Fox's cunning is trumped, and laughter and applause close the reading.

Engaged and fluent reading performances, like the one in which Juanita participated, came from children who weeks before read haltingly and without confidence. For 10 weeks, their language arts instruction included daily Readers Theatre experiences aimed toward increasing the children's oral reading fluency. Because their practices were "rehearsals," rereadings were both purposeful and fun. At the end of the 10 weeks, these second graders had made reading gains that were significantly greater than students in comparison classrooms.

As many teachers know, Readers Theatre is an interpretive reading activity in which readers use their voices to bring characters to life. Unlike conventional theater, Readers Theatre requires no sets, costumes, props, or memorized lines. Rather, the performer's goal is to read a script aloud effectively, enabling the audience to visualize the action. Besides the characters, the narrator has a special role in Readers Theatre. Narrators provide the cementing details and explanations that may be found in the original text's narration, descriptions, or even illustrations. Although we realized Readers Theatre has been used to encourage students' appreciation of literature and eagerness to read, we were interested in the influence of Readers Theatre on the fluency of second-grade students who need more practice to make their hesitant reading more fluid.

Defining Fluency

Although most teachers have fluency as one of their goals for children's reading, they frequently find it a struggle to explain what fluency is. As one teacher observed, "I don't know how to define it, but I know it when I hear it." Others offer explanations that are logical, yet incomplete: "Fluency is reading at a good pace." "Fluent reading is reading without errors." "It's reading with expression."

Even investigators who have looked closely at oral reading fluency don't seem to agree. Some have inspected rate (e.g., Chomsky, 1976; Dahl & Samuels, 1974). Some have broadened the lens to include accuracy as well as rate in their inspections of fluency (e.g., LaBerge & Samuels, 1979). Still others have looked at phrasing (e.g., Schreiber, 1980) or the use of prosodic features

Reprinted from Martinez, M., Roser, N.L., & Strecker, S. (1998). "I never thought I could be a star": A Readers Theatre ticket to fluency. *The Reading Teacher, 52*(4), 326–334.

such as pitch, stress, pauses, and expressiveness (e.g., Dowhower, 1987; Herman, 1985). We considered each of these indicators when we inspected fluency. If demonstration of fluency depends upon appropriate rate, accuracy, phrasing, and expression, we wondered whether Readers Theatre had potential to orchestrate all these fluency components.

What Fluency Instruction Looks Like

There are both logical arguments and observational evidence that Readers Theatre can support instruction in reading fluency. That is, the individual instructional features of Readers Theatre have already been associated with growth in fluency both in studies and teachers' testimonies.

Access to Manageable Materials

Students who are becoming fluent readers need manageable texts in which to practice (Allington, 1983; Rasinski, 1989; Zutell & Rasinski, 1991). The reading selection itself is an important element in building fluency. First, it's important to choose texts for Readers Theatre that are within the reader's reach. By definition, text within a reader's instructional range reduces word recognition demands and allows for more rapid reading. As rate increases, the reader is able to devote more attention to meaning and the interpretation of meaning through phrasing and expressiveness. That is, accuracy, rate, phrasing, and expressiveness are all depressed when the text is too difficult.

Second, work within the world of oral interpretation suggests that stories with certain features are more easily adapted to Readers Theatre. Stories with straightforward plots that present characters grappling with dilemmas requiring thought and talk can easily be turned into scripts. For example, a strong script is likely to result from a story like Marc Brown's *Arthur Babysits* in which the main character grapples with an ethical dilemma. By contrast, a story like Alexei Tolstoy's *The Great Big Enormous Turnip* with sprawling, boisterous action begs for

enactment; it almost demands that children form a chain to pull up that turnip rather than read the story from stools at the front of the room.

Third, Readers Theatre can also build on children's enthusiasm for series books. Feitelson, Kita, and Goldstein (1986) found that familiar story characters and settings are more easily grasped and better understood by young children. Similarly, if children meet the same characters in script after script, those characters become much like friends who have shared many different experiences. They can anticipate those recurring characters' reactions—even to new situations. When it's time to step into those characters' shoes, the children's portrayals of the characters become increasingly believable.

Effective Reading Models

To know what fluent reading "sounds like," students need to hear effective models (e.g., Bear & Cathey, 1989; Eldredge, 1990; Hoffman, 1987). Sometimes teachers request, "Read that again with expression," but children don't always know what expressive reading is. By listening to good models of fluent reading, students can hear how a reader's voice makes text make sense. That understanding, more than exaggerated voice inflection, is the basis for expressiveness. When teachers read aloud the stories on which Readers Theatre scripts are based, teachers guide students into the sounds and meanings of those stories.

Rereadings

Students who have opportunities for repeatedly reading the same texts become fluent (e.g., Dahl & Samuels, 1974; Dowhower, 1987; Reutzel & Hollingsworth, 1993). Teachers have understood for a long time that reading stories repeatedly improves fluency (as in Samuels, 1979). Chall (1983) argues that children at about second-grade level *choose* to read repeatedly for the sheer joy of becoming proficient. No longer glued to print, they "take off" in reading. People who observe these readers note their love of riddles and jokes and almost any kind of text that lends itself to being read aloud often. Hickman (1979) found that second and third graders were far less likely to want to talk about stories than younger or older children because they were so intent on practicing their craft. As 7-year-old Erin explained it, "It's like getting the training wheels off your bicycle. You just ride and ride and ride. Now I got reading. I just read and read and read."

Instructional Support and Feedback

Students who receive instruction and feedback are more likely to develop reading fluency (Koskinen & Blum, 1986; Rasinski, 1989). Students can gain insights into how to become more fluent readers by talking with their teachers and peers about how good readers sound. Immature readers sometimes describe good reading as "knowing every word" or "reading fast." With guidance, they come to understand that good oral reading also involves bringing the text to life by producing a defensible interpretation. Guidance can occur informally as teacher and children talk about a just-completed performance, or it can be a more planned demonstration of a strategy that fluent readers use.

Into the Classroom With Readers Theatre

Given what we understood about fluency instruction, we introduced an instructional model for 30-minute daily sessions in Readers Theatre. The two second-grade classes that participated in the project were in inner-city school districts. One class was composed of Hispanic children of low socioeconomic status; the other was an ethnically mixed group from varying socioeconomic backgrounds.

Choosing the Texts

Because the children in each classroom were at a range of reading levels, we looked for books of varying difficulty level, so that each child could meet with text within his or her instructional range. We looked for a body of works—a series—with interesting characters who meet ponderable dilemmas to ensure that children would come to know the characters well and thoroughly. We wanted texts that would provide a sufficient number (four or five) of recurring roles. In addition, we sought humorous texts.

For the lower level readers in the two classes, we chose Marshall's Fox series (for example, *Fox on Stage*, *Fox in Love*). The mid-range readers read scripts based on Marc Brown's Arthur series. We didn't find a series that seemed a perfect fit with the upper level readers in the two classrooms, so we chose, instead, a set of related books—tongue-in-cheek fairy tales written or illustrated by James Marshall (e.g., *Hansel and Gretel*, *Cinderella*). We knew this meant that the best second-grade readers in these classes wouldn't be meeting the same characters repeatedly (as would the other students), but the books they read were stylistically similar and the tales themselves were familiar ones. As soon as the groups were formed, they became three "repertory companies" and carried that designation throughout the project.

Preparing the Scripts

The books were recast as Readers Theatre scripts with only these changes: Brief narration was added when necessary to describe story action revealed only by an illustration. Long narrations were sometimes divided into two speaking parts (Narrators 1 and 2). A portion of a script appears in Figure 1.

For every book we made two copies of each script for each child. The first copy was carried home so that each child could practice each of the speaking parts throughout the week. The second script, the "at-school" copy, had each character's speaking parts highlighted with neon markers. Teachers collected these second copies at the end of each day's practice session. During the week's rehearsals, children would pass along both the script and the role they had just read. Once the performance day's role was decided upon, however, they held on to the script with their own lines highlighted.

Organizing the Repertory Groups

The three repertory groups were organized in each classroom and each group read scripts based on texts written at appropriate levels of difficulty. Like real repertory companies, the players faced the challenge of regularly rehearsing new material (in this case, each week). The groups had a practice routine, and each player was asked to take on different roles each week. In some instances, a player even had to take on more than one part in a production. Again, like real repertory groups, the players knew they were rehearsing for a real audience. The companies staked their rehearsal areas in the corners of the classrooms. Their weekly instructional and performance routines are described in the sections that follow.

The Weekly Routine

Every Monday morning, the children looked forward to hearing their teacher read three new stories aloud. These were the stories on which the week's Readers Theatre scripts would be based. Because the teacher had practiced each story, as each was read aloud, the teacher made a special effort to interpret it in ways that would bring the story to life. After the second graders talked about the content and meaning of the stories, the teacher presented a minilesson designed to demonstrate and make explicit some aspect of fluent reading. For example, one lesson focused on why and when a good reader might need to slow down or speed up. In another, students discussed how a reader uses the circumstances a character faces to decide how to convey that character's feelings. As a result of those lessons, when Maria played the role of Arthur in Marc Brown's *Arthur Meets the President*, her interpretation of Arthur's speech at the White House began slowly and painfully, "Good afternoon, Mr. President. When I think…about…what…I…can…do…to…make America…great…ah, ah, ah…." Maria explained her slow reading: "I know Arthur is embarrassed. He can't remember what he wants to say. Everyone is looking at him. Arthur hates that. His words are stuck."

Following the minilesson, the teacher distributed copies of the three scripts to the repertory groups. The students practiced reading the scripts either independently or with a buddy. At the end of the session, the children were encouraged to take their copy of the script home to do more practicing that night and through the week.

On Tuesday, the students gathered in their respective repertory groups. The teacher passed out the second set of scripts to each group. On this set, specific parts were highlighted in color. Children practiced reading as a "company" for the first time. When they finished, the children passed their scripts to the left so that each ended up with a new script and a new role to practice. Rehearsal began again. The teacher circulated among the three groups, coaching and providing feedback. Coaching sounded like this:

- "Remember that D.W. just rode her bike for the first time. How do you think she might sound?"
- "Could you read that again and pause for the comma? Let's see if it makes more sense."
- "I noticed how you 'punched' the word *never* in that sentence. That really helps the listener get the meaning."

Feedback also came from other players and felt much like the collaboration found in Author's Chair: "Here's what I liked about the way Jazz read Arthur's part..." Scripts continued to be read and passed until the end of the session.

Wednesday's routines were exactly like Tuesday's. That is, students rehearsed by reading the highlighted part and then exchanging scripts to practice another role. In the final 5 minutes of the session, signaled by the teacher, students in each repertory company learned to negotiate and quickly determine roles for Friday's audience performance. The teacher encouraged the children to pay special attention to their performance role when they practiced their at-home copy of the script.

On Thursday, students spent the session working together reading and rereading their performance roles in preparation for the next day's production. During the final few minutes, students sometimes made character labels and discussed where each would stand during Readers Theatre performance.

By Friday, each performer was ready, having, on average, read the script or the story 15–20 times. Every week each repertory group performed before a live audience. The audience varied; some weeks the repertory groups read in other classrooms. Parents were sometimes invited for the performance. The principal, school librarian, or counselor were frequently in the audience. At other times, the class itself served as audience, as one repertory company read in front of the other two groups. There was great anticipation as to who the week's audience would be. The children themselves made lots of eager suggestions. "The audience effect was important," explained Ms. Carter, one of the teachers who participated in the study. "The anticipation of an audience is what made reading practice seem like a dress rehearsal."

As for "classroom management," the children settled fairly rapidly into the routines of their repertory group. At first, there were some warm exchanges about coveted roles, even though teachers made it clear that everyone would play every role, and that continuing roles would be rotated. Manuscript passing, role assignment, and turn-taking soon became routine. Like the procedures for Author's Chair, the routines for repertory groups (see Figure 2) became automatic, so that the focus moved toward smoothing the performance, as well as on enjoyment and showmanship.

What Children Gained From Readers Theatre

We made pre- and postassessments of students' oral readings of unrehearsed stories from the same or similar series we had used in the repertory groups. Over the 10-week project, nearly all of the children posted gains in their rate of reading. Some of these gains were dramatic. For example, Victoria read her pre-project text at 74 words per minute. By the end of the project, she read at 125 words per minute. Similarly, Rebecca's rate grew from 40 to 88 words per minute. Overall, there was an average rate increase of 17 words per minute for these second graders, while two similar classes of second graders who had the series books in their classroom libraries, but no Readers Theatre, gained an average of 6.9 words per minute. Even so, Readers Theatre experiences didn't affect the rate of every child. We puzzled over Patricia, for example, whose rate stayed exactly the same over the 10-week period. Hasbrouck and Tindal (1992) hold that 78 words per minute is an expected rate for second graders. Given that standard, 76% of our group fell below at the outset, yet at the end of 10 weeks, 75% had approached or exceeded the standard.

Gains in accuracy told us less. That may be because the materials "fit" the students at the

Figure 2
A 5-Day Instructional Plan for Readers Theatre

Pre-Day 1	Teacher chooses stories and develops scripts for each text.
Day 1	• Teacher models fluency by reading aloud the stories on which the week's scripts are based. • Teacher offers a brief minilesson that presents explicit explanation of some aspect of fluency. • The teacher and students discuss each of the three stories. • Students begin to practice reading personal copies of scripts, reading all the parts independently. • Teacher encourages students to take these unmarked scripts home for further practice.
Day 2	• Students gather in repertory groups. Teacher provides scripts for each group with specific parts highlighted. • Students read the script, taking a different part with each reading. • Teacher circulates among the three repertory groups, coaching and providing feedback.
Day 3	• Procedures are the same as for Day 2. • During the final 5 minutes, students within each repertory group negotiate and assign roles for Day 5's performance. • Teacher encourages children to pay special attention to their newly assigned performance role when practicing at home.
Day 4	• Students read and reread the parts to which they are assigned within their repertory groups. • During the final 10 minutes, students make character labels and discuss where each will stand during the performance.
Day 5	• Repertory groups "perform," reading before an audience.

outset. Each student's accuracy was already at an acceptable—or instructional—level. They got better, but there was little room to show accuracy growth in these texts. There were also gains in reading levels on the Informal Reading Inventories administered prior to the beginning of the project and at the project's end. For the children for whom all data were available, 9 gained two grade levels, and 14 gained one grade level. Only 5 children showed no reading level gain. Across the hall, in the two comparison classrooms, 3 children gained two grade levels; 13 gained one grade level, and 12 showed no gain in reading level.

We used a 5-point scale to rate students' fluidity, phrasing, and expressiveness of oral reading on the pre- and postassessments. This analysis documented improvement for all but 4 of the children. The remaining children improved in at least one facet of oral reading fluency, with most improving in two or even three facets. In comparison groups, 10 of the 28 children showed no improvement in oral reading fluency. The children who did show growth typically did so in only one facet of fluency (e.g., phrasing).

Readers Theatre seemed especially well suited to helping children go "inside" the story, experiencing the thoughts and feelings of the characters. As we observed in the two classrooms, we witnessed many instances of this. Sometimes a teacher probe assisted students in contemplating the meaning of a scene: "How is James Marshall's *Goldilocks* different from other Goldilocks? How can the voice of Goldilocks give the audience a clue to that difference?" At other times students themselves initiated discussion regarding oral interpretation that delved into comprehension on a deep level, as evidenced in this interaction about *Hansel and Gretel* (Marshall, 1990).

Vicky: Your voice is too sweet. I don't think Gretel would talk nice to her stepmother.

Jessica: That's what I'm doing. Gretel is being *too* sweet because she can't stand her. I want it to sound like phony, not like I'm really trying to be nice.

As expected, we found that the series books promoted familiarity with characters' personae. For example, Arthur's friend Francine was interpreted as a know-it-all smarty pants every week, regardless of the performer. Children also learned to expect certain types of story situations to occur in the series books. Leaving the classroom one Friday afternoon, Daniel called back, "I can't wait to see what trouble Fox gets in next week!" Such expectations for story can serve as a solid basis for interpreting future stories through Readers Theatre.

The teachers, Ms. Carter and Mr. Meneses, also attended to their students' enthusiasm for Readers Theatre. Reading practice as "rehearsal" proved to be a motivational method to encourage repeated readings. The "lure of performance" (Busching, 1981, p. 34) offered an incentive for returning to the text again and again, as students worked to bring the written words to life for Friday's audience. Ms. Carter explained the pervading influence of the scripts in classroom life: "They read those [original] books during their reading time. They wrote about the books and their own plays based on the same characters. They wrote story extensions of the scripts. They also invited their parents to attend performances and repeatedly asked, 'Is it time for Readers Theatre?'" We found further evidence of the motivational power of Readers Theatre in the students' writing journals. Omar wrote, "Readers theater is the funnest reading I've ever did before!" Lucia wrote, "I never thought I could be a star, but I was the BEST reader today."

Conclusions

Readers Theatre seems to offer teachers a way to incorporate repeated readings within a meaningful and purposeful context. Creating opportunities for students to perform before an audience requires multiple readings of the text in order to achieve the fluency needed for the performance, and that practice works. Ms. Carter summarized the benefits: "I see two reasons why Readers Theatre helped my students so much. The first is comprehension that results from having to become the characters and understand their feelings, and the second is the repetition and practice." Encouraging appropriate oral interpretation not only assists students with their expressiveness, but also sharpens their insights into the literature for themselves and their listeners. As Coger (1963) states, "The study of the written page becomes fun, and reading it aloud deepens the reader's understanding of the text, for in reading it aloud the readers experience the writing more deeply" (p. 322).

Preparing a reading for an audience is a powerful incentive for reading practice. We observed the energy of students performing for a new audience. We observed changes in levels of confidence that a well-rehearsed effort produces. We also observed the changes in popularity of the books in the classroom library, and students who were content to just "read and read and read." They never seemed to tire of perfecting their craft.

Readers Theatre, then, offers a reason for children to read repeatedly in appropriate materials. It provides a vehicle for direct explanation, feedback, and effective modeling. Perhaps due to the interplay of these influences, we found that Readers Theatre promoted oral reading fluency, as children explored and interpreted the meanings of literature (with joy)!

Authors' Note

We would like to thank Claire Carter and Ed Meneses for sharing their insights about Readers Theatre.

References

Allington, R.L. (1983). Fluency: The neglected goal. *The Reading Teacher*, *36*, 556–561.

Bear, D., & Cathey, S. (1989, November). *Writing and reading fluency and orthographic awareness.* Paper presented at the meeting of the National Reading Conference, Tucson, AZ.

Busching, B. (1981). Readers' theater: An education for language and life. *Language Arts*, *58*, 330–338.

Chall, J.S. (1983). *Stages of reading development.* New York: McGraw-Hill.

Chomsky, C. (1976). After decoding: What? *Language Arts*, *53*, 374–390.

Coger, L.I. (1963). Theatre for oral interpreters. *Speech Teacher*, *12*, 322–330.

Dahl, P.R., & Samuels, S.J. (1974). *A mastery based experimental program for teaching poor readers high speed word recognition skills.* Unpublished manuscript, University of Minnesota, Minneapolis.

Dowhower, S.L. (1987). Effect of repeated reading on second grade transitional readers' fluency and comprehension. *Reading Research Quarterly*, *22*, 389–406.

Eldredge, J.L. (1990). *An experiment using a group assisted repeated reading strategy with poor readers.* Unpublished manuscript, Brigham Young University, Provo, UT. (ERIC Document Reproduction Service No. ED 314 721)

Feitelson, D., Kita, B., & Goldstein, Z. (1986). Effects of listening to series stories on first graders' comprehension and use of language. *Research in the Teaching of English*, *20*, 339–356.

Hasbrouck, J.E., & Tindal, G. (1992). Curriculum-based oral reading fluency norms for students in grades 2 through 5. *Teaching Exceptional Children*, *24*, 41–44.

Herman, P.A. (1985). The effect of repeated readings on reading rate, speech pauses, and word recognition accuracy. *Reading Research Quarterly*, *20*, 553–564.

Hickman, J.G. (1979). *Response to literature in a school environment, grades K–5.* Unpublished doctoral dissertation, The Ohio State University, Columbus.

Hoffman, J.V. (1987). Rethinking the role of oral reading in basal instruction. *Elementary School Journal*, *87*, 367–374.

Koskinen, P.A., & Blum, I.H. (1986). Paired repeated reading: A classroom strategy for developing fluent reading. *The Reading Teacher*, *40*, 70–75.

LaBerge, D., & Samuels, S.J. (1979). Toward a theory of automatic information processing in reading. *Cognitive Psychology*, *6*, 293–323.

Rasinski, T.V. (1989). Fluency for everyone: Incorporating fluency instruction in the classroom. *The Reading Teacher*, *42*, 690–693.

Reutzel, D.R., & Hollingsworth, P.M. (1993). Effects of fluency training on second graders' reading comprehension. *Journal of Educational Research*, *86*, 325–331.

Samuels, S.J. (1979). The method of repeated reading. *The Reading Teacher*, *32*, 403–408.

Schreiber, P.A. (1980). On the acquisition of reading fluency. *Journal of Reading Behavior*, *12*, 177–186.

Zutell, J., & Rasinski, T. (1991). Training teachers to attend to their students' oral reading fluency. *Theory Into Practice*, *30*, 212–217.

Children's Books Cited

Brown, M. (1991). *Arthur meets the president.* Boston: Little, Brown.

Brown, M. (1992). *Arthur babysits.* Boston: Little, Brown.

Karlin, B. (1992). *Cinderella.* Ill. J. Marshall. Boston: Little, Brown.

Marshall, E. (1994). *Fox in love.* Ill. J. Marshall. New York: Puffin.

Marshall, J. (1990). *Hansel and Gretel.* New York: Dial.

Marshall, J. (1993). *Fox on stage.* New York: Puffin.

Tolstoy, A. (1968). *The great big enormous turnip.* London: Piccolo.

Questions for Reflection

- Many children do enjoy performing in front of an audience, but some are less enthusiastic. In what ways can you support Readers Theatre performances for your shy or nervous students, so that they will be successful and grow in fluency and reading confidence as a result of their participation?

- The authors describe careful selection of books to serve as the source of scripts for readers at different ability levels. What sort of additional consideration might need to be given to selection of texts for students who are English-language learners?

- This article describes using Readers Theatre as an activity in second grade. What benefits might exist for Readers Theatre in upper elementary, middle, or secondary grades? How might the activity be modified for use with older learners?

A Focus on Fluency: How One Teacher Incorporated Fluency With Her Reading Curriculum

Lorraine Wiebe Griffith and Timothy V. Rasinski

Reading fluency is the ability to read accurately, quickly, effortlessly, and with appropriate expression and meaning (Rasinski, 2003). The National Reading Panel identified it as a key ingredient in successful reading instruction (National Institute of Child Health and Human Development, 2000). Reading fluency is important because it affects students' reading efficiency and comprehension.

The theory of automaticity in reading (LaBerge & Samuels, 1974) provides a theoretical explanation for the importance of reading fluency. According to this theory, readers have a limited amount of attention they can devote to cognitive tasks such as reading. Reading requires readers to accomplish at least two critical tasks—they must decode the words and comprehend the text. Given the limited amount of attentional resources available to any reader, attention that is given to the decoding requirement cannot be used for comprehension. Thus, readers who must spend considerable cognitive effort to decode words, even if they are successful at that task, may compromise their comprehension because they are not able to devote a sufficient amount of their attention to making sense of the text.

One fluency goal for reading instruction then is to develop decoding to the point where it becomes an automatic process that requires a minimum of attention. When decoding and the other surface-level aspects of reading are automatized, readers can devote a maximal amount of attention to the deeper levels of reading—comprehension. A second dimension (theoretical explanation) of reading fluency lies in the role of prosodic or expressive reading (Schreiber, 1980, 1987, 1991; Schreiber & Read, 1980). Fluent readers not only are appropriately fast but also read with good phrasing and expression—they are able to express or embed meaning into the text through their oral interpretation of the passage. In this sense, then, as students learn to read in an expressive and meaningful manner they are also learning to construct meaning or comprehend the text. A recent review of the research related to reading fluency confirms that fluency is indeed a significant factor in reading and is related to comprehension and achievement (Kuhn & Stahl, 2000).

Although fluency has been identified as a key element in successful reading programs, it is often not a significant part of them (Allington, 1983; Rasinski & Zutell, 1996). When I (Timothy, second author) speak about reading fluency to groups of teachers, I usually receive comments from participants that fluency is not something that was taught in their teacher training programs and that it is not part of their implemented reading curriculum—in short, they indicate a lack of familiarity with the concept of fluency and how best to teach it.

When I talk with teachers about reading fluency, I often hear later from many of them about

Reprinted from Griffith, L.W., & Rasinski, T.V. (2004). A focus on fluency: How one teacher incorporated fluency with her reading curriculum. *The Reading Teacher, 58*(2), 126–137.

what they are trying in the way of fluency instruction. Lorraine Griffith (first author) is one of those teachers. Since her initial contact with me over three years ago, we have often corresponded about reading instruction in general and reading fluency in particular. What she has done to make reading fluency an integral part of her curriculum has been, in my opinion, exceptional and a great example of classroom scholarship. In this article we share how she has transformed her reading program by incorporating fluency instruction into the curriculum.

Critically Thinking Nonreaders

Year after year, children have streamed into my (Lorraine's) rural fourth-grade classroom reading below grade level. Teaching in North Carolina, USA, a high-stakes assessment state, I felt the increasing pressure to pull them up efficiently and effectively. I used a combination of silent reading, partner reading, and teacher read-alouds in my guided reading instruction. Students discussed their silent, independent reading with me and with their classmates. I included classroom instruction to be sure my kids were prepared with the best comprehension tools—multiple-choice questions at multiple levels of depth and question stems from sample lists provided by the North Carolina Department of Public Instruction. I worked hard on having students think about their thinking, learn about inference, and make judgments on text.

From the year before I began embedding a fluency emphasis into my curriculum (1999), I have a vivid memory of a lanky girl named Ally (all names used in this article are pseudonyms). At the beginning of fourth grade she could successfully read a first-grade level word list and comprehend at a 2.5 level while reading silently on an informal reading inventory. Because of an apparent phonics deficit, her Title I teacher (part of a federally funded program intended to help disadvantaged children at risk of school failure) worked with her one-on-one in phonics for 30 minutes a day for the entire school year. To nurture her reading comprehension, I used think-alouds in whole-class instruction on a regular basis.

During test-preparation remediation time, my student teacher, the remediation assistant, or I would take Ally alone and read the test-prep article aloud to save time, due to Ally's slow and labored reading. We would then model critical thinking through thinking aloud the question and finding cues in the text to help answer. Ally seemed to make terrific progress, eventually answering about 80% of questions correctly on grade-level passages. At year's end, Ally had also shown progress in the Title I testing. She was able to successfully read a fourth-grade level word list, a three-year gain. In contrast, she came up only six months, to a third-grade level, in silent reading comprehension. When the state testing rolled around, Ally was unable to pass. Tears rolled down her face as she looked up at me during the first break, unable to finish even the first long article of the test. The state testing required more from the students: to decode longer passages effectively and with automaticity and to answer higher level questions of analysis and synthesis. We had focused on helping her to decode efficiently and to think critically about text we had read aloud to her, but the actual skill of independent reading and comprehending simultaneously was still missing from her set of reading skills and strategies.

As I reflected on my practice, I realized the at-risk readers, children whose silent reading comprehension levels were below fourth grade, were probably more dependent on the teacher read-alouds during guided reading or a picture-enhanced text than on the independently read, grade-level texts themselves. If I didn't read the text aloud, they would depend on the class discussion and summary of the text for basic comprehension before answering the multiple-choice questions. My students were fooling me throughout the school year because they were participating actively in our class discussions. They could develop ideas, extend thoughts, and appear to have fully comprehended the text when they were simply building on other people's reading abilities.

I knew I needed a better strategy for closing the reading gap. To date, my at-risk fourth graders had averaged a 1.2-year gain in silent reading according to the informal reading inventory used in our Title I program. In order for children who are up to three years below grade level to catch up by middle school, the reading gains needed to increase significantly. The catch-up plan needed to be more than just effective—it needed to be efficient. My instructional day was already full, with use of a balanced literacy model, so I could consider substituting changes in practice only during the existing blocks of time.

A Strategy Shift to Fluency With Readers Theatre: Year 1

In July 2000, I heard Tim Rasinski speak on "Strategies for Struggling Readers" at a local district-supported workshop. I was struck by the data he reported on fluency and especially by one of the studies he discussed from *The Reading Teacher* article "I Never Thought I Could Be a Star: A Readers Theatre Ticket to Reading Fluency" (Martinez, Roser, & Strecker, 1999). I was amazed to see the second graders in the study make remarkable progress in their reading comprehension after only a 10-week implementation of an authentic oral reading fluency strategy—Readers Theatre.

I knew that the eventual goal of reading instruction was for children to be able to think critically about text they read silently. I wanted them to be able to read a text independently, comprehending it deeply enough to answer questions requiring judgment and analysis of text. But there was a step missing in my reading instruction between decoding text and being able to critically think about that text. Somehow I had to find a way to bridge the gap between a stumbling grasp of independent reading with most of the child's attention focused on decoding, to a firm grip on the deeper, interpretive skill that accompanies fluent reading with understanding.

I was ready to try a shift in my reading instruction techniques to an emphasis on fluency instruction. I decided to emulate the study I had heard and read about (Martinez et al., 1999) and try Readers Theatre for the first 10 weeks of the 2000–2001 school year.

Because I was not sure this idea warranted radical changes in a fourth-grade classroom, I did not alter my guided reading block. I continued to use a varied combination of novels, short stories, nonfiction, and the basal reader as texts. I continued to teach the same critical thinking techniques in discussion of real text. But I added an emphasis on reading fluency through Readers Theatre using minimal classroom time.

Finding Scripts

Before I could begin implementation in my classroom, I had to locate Readers Theatre scripts. At first I wondered how I would find enough scripts to keep my children reading for 10 weeks. I was amazed to find free Readers Theatre scripts on Internet sites, such as Aaron Shepard's (www.aaronshep.com/rt/index.html). I also found a number of age-appropriate script collections for purchase and especially enjoyed the scripts by Braun and Braun (2000a, 2000b) and Dixon, Davies, and Politano (1996). But I soon discovered that scripts were quite easy to develop on my own, especially when using poetry such as Maya Angelou's poem "Life Doesn't Frighten Me at All" (Angelou & Basquiat, 1998). Moving beyond poetry into content-related topics, I found that scripts I arranged could be integrated quite effectively with language arts, science, or social studies.

One example of a Readers Theatre script I developed is "Magnetism" (Figure 1), to be used in conjunction with an electricity unit. I simply pulled key phrases from a nonfiction text and then added some similes for literary value. My goal was to introduce some of the key vocabulary and concepts in the unit and also have the children think about the deeper meaning of magnetism removed from the context of science.

Weekly Procedure

I followed a simple weekly procedure. In the beginning weeks, every child had the same script.

I wanted the more accomplished readers to model fluent reading for the others. After copying enough scripts for each child, I highlighted the assigned parts using a variety of colored highlighters. I quickly and randomly handed out the highlighted Readers Theatre scripts on Monday mornings and assigned a nightly 10-minute practice read. The children recorded their practice times in reading logs, usually rehearsing with a parent or sibling. On Fridays, just before lunchtime, the children rehearsed in groups for about 15 minutes. Because each child received a script randomly with only his or her part actually marked, and then practiced independently during the week, they actually "met" their fellow performers just before lunch on Fridays during rehearsal. The highlighted parts had been color-coded so I could just announce, "Pink group practice by the windows...yellow group near the computers." While they practiced, I coached individuals and small groups of students in reading with expression and meaning.

The nature of Readers Theatre requires interpretation of text with the human voice. There is no memorization of text because the children are asked to creatively interpret the meaning of the passage each time they read. There is no acting; there are no props and no costumes. The drama is communicated by the children, through phrasing, pausing, and expressive reading of text.

Initially, it was effective to have all of the children use the same script. One child would see her or his part interpreted a number of different ways and recognize the potential drama in the written word. As the weeks went on I developed a wider variety of script resources. Eventually I divided the children into different performance troupes each week. Each group of readers had a different script to perform, allowing for a much more interesting Friday production. But I paid no attention to the child's reading level as I assigned parts. It was truly a nonability-grouped activity. Because the text was practiced so often throughout the week and the lines were limited in number, even a low-functioning reader could perform well on Friday. I wanted all of the children to consider themselves as equals during the performances, differing only on the level of dramatic interpretation of the texts. I found that some of my lower level readers were the most dramatic, in their first opportunity ever to shine as star performers in reading.

Our grade level traditionally had enjoyed a "Fun Friday" reward time on Friday afternoons. All week long I would arrange for the celebration. The students would engage in fun activities such as cooking or watching a movie that correlated with the unit of study. With a new group of students at the beginning of a new school year, I announced that we would have a special celebration of reading every Friday afternoon. To make the performance a special occasion, the children took turns bringing in refreshments. They were thrilled with Fridays and loved to perform in a "dinner theater" atmosphere. I had managed to substitute a meaningful reading intervention for a mishmash of other activities. The time I used to spend on finding varieties of flavored puddings to represent the layers of the earth I now spent finding more Readers Theatre scripts related to our studies.

In only 10 weeks, I saw positive results similar to the second-grade study I had attempted to emulate. But I also saw a deepened interest in reading. I began to see expressiveness emerge from the children's oral reading during the guided reading block. I was actually seeing reading redefined and reading interest renewed by the students in my class. At one point while partner reading "Why Frog and Snake Never Play Together" (Bryan, 1989) during guided reading, one of my English-language learners whispered to another struggling reader, "Let's read that part again, only this time like Readers Theatre." In all of my years teaching fourth grade, I had never heard a child come up with the idea to reread a passage simply for the pleasure of reading it.

Thrilled with the initial 10-week progress, I decided to continue with a fluency emphasis and to keep data for the rest of the school year. Because we were a Title I school and my greatest concern was with the at-risk children who were not learning disabled but were reading significantly below grade level, I was able to take advantage of the Title I testing program for the targeted students. I had not seen a yearlong study of the effect of Readers Theatre on at-risk students in the intermediate grades and wondered if the reading enthusiasm and emphasis on expressive flow would last. I also wondered what kind of impact it would make on testing with the Title I students over a full school year.

After the first year of implementation, my own observations of reading growth were confirmed as my four targeted Title I students experienced a 2.5-year increase in their silent reading comprehension as measured by an informal reading inventory. I was thrilled to find that this relatively brief and simple intervention had more than doubled the gain I might normally have expected students to make in one year of instruction. Even with a lessened stress on phonics instruction during the 30-minute Title I block and a greater stress on reading with meaning and expression, the children's average gain in word-list recognition was 1.25 years, substantively more than in previous years.

A Continued Shift to Fluency Development: Year 2

Feeling wildly enthusiastic about the improvement of more than a year simply by using Readers Theatre to focus on fluency, I continued my quest for a deepened understanding of fluency development. I had read Timothy Rasinski's (2000) article in *The Reading Teacher* entitled "Speed Does Matter in Reading," and during the 2001–2002 year I decided to investigate the role of reading rate in a child's reading comprehension. I tested my children's reading rate by doing one-minute reading probes. The methodology was simple: I had the children read a grade-level passage and recorded notes on words omitted or pronounced incorrectly and counted the words read correctly. I was surprised to find out that 44% of my children read below the normal reading rate of 99 words correct per minute for the beginning of fourth grade (Rasinski, 2003). Fifteen percent of my children were at risk, reading below 74 words correct per minute.

I decided to keep track of the reading rate of all of my children and the silent reading comprehension of my five Title I students (see Table 1). I also began experimenting with the implementation of two other interventions to increase reading fluency: short-term use of timed reads and selective partner reading.

Timed Reads

Having read a book on using "writer's craft passages" as an integral part of the writing block (Fletcher & Portalupi, 1998), I selected exemplary passages from children's trade books that were to be used for writing each week. As a fourth-grade teacher in North Carolina, I also felt the pressure to improve writing test scores. I was convinced that using authentic text written by published and award-winning authors as models of writing was the best way to teach narrative writing. So after continuing to study the idea of writer's craft (Ray, 1999), I realized there was a tie-in between the passages for writing and the passages for repeated reading. Having the children practice read the passages taken from trade books would cement the vocabulary and writing techniques with their thinking about writing.

For the first week of using the timed reads, I ran copies from the opening scene of *Roll of Thunder, Hear My Cry* (Taylor, 1976). I read the passage aloud to the children with attention to the syntax and expressive nature (see Figure 2).

After doing a minilesson on the characterization of "Little Man," we discussed the author's style of writing and the way the author opened with such a telling statement about Little Man. We talked about how we could use that technique of character description to open our own stories.

	Reading rate (one-minute probe using a cold 4.0-level passage each time)	Silent reading comprehension (Qualitative Reading Inventory-II)*
Table 1 **Gains in Fluency and Comprehension for the Five At-Risk (Title I) Students in Lorraine's Classroom, 2001-2002 School Year**		
Beginning of fourth grade (August 2001)	62.4 words correct per minute	2.2 grade level
Middle of fourth grade (January 2002)	103.8 words correct per minute (+41.4 words correct per minute)	4.8 grade level (+2.6 years)
End of fourth grade (April 2002)	109.8 words correct per minute (+6.8 words correct per minute)	5.4 grade level (+0.6 years)

*Testing was conducted by a third party.

The following day the children each read the 120-word passage to a partner for one minute and made a mark in the passage where they ended reading. After each child had read, we discussed the way different children read the passage. I chose students to "model read" for the class to demonstrate expressive and interpretive reading.

We then moved on to using the same passage as a model for writing narrative. Building on this passage from *Roll of Thunder, Hear My Cry*, I had the children do webs of descriptive words of a younger child they knew, and then write creative first sentences that might hook a reader. Analyzing a passage and then using an author's technique to write helped the children develop writing fluency and creativity. But because our accompanying goal was rereading for increased reading fluency, we read the same passage daily through the week. The children noted their increasing reading rate each day, and we talked about how important reading with energy and enthusiasm is to understanding what we read.

The children loved competing against themselves each day and recording the number of words they could read expressively in one minute. The children were cautioned not to read as fast as they could for the sake of reading fast but rather to read with expression and meaning. Students began to internalize the characteristics of the writer's techniques and vocabulary as they practiced reading again and again. There were times when the oral interpretation of an author's passage was so moving I had to hold back tears. I was seeing the benefits of theatrical performance interwoven with this emphasis on reading fluency and writer's craft. As one student commented, "When you write you think of the good words and expression sort of comes to your head. It makes your story better if you have good expression in it."

Partner Reading

Children reading at or above grade level read orally with partners during the daily 30-minute Title I block. The Title I teacher sometimes worked with a small group reading novels and encouraged children to read aloud as they desired. But she also covered skills necessary for the understanding of text through programs used in our district. The rest of the children read in pairs or small groups of similar reading levels. The book chosen by each pair would be read together orally at school and then continued silently at home. A few of the children in Title I requested to move into partner reading with their friends, simply reading the whole 30 minutes instead of having the small-group time. This request was usually granted because for the first time these at-risk children desired to participate in a reading culture; they were beginning to realize a social dimension to reading. During this particular block, I conferred with the reading pairs about their selections.

During the 2001–2002 school year, the additional short-term interventions of timed readings, repeated readings, and encouraging reading at a higher rate and with expression seemed to have a direct impact on word recognition and silent reading comprehension. Title I

Figure 2
Excerpt From *Roll of Thunder, Hear My Cry*

"Little Man, would you come on? You keep it up and you're gonna make us late."... He lagged several feet behind my other brothers, Stacey and Christopher-John, and me, attempting to keep the rusty Mississippi dust from swelling with each step and drifting back upon his shiny black shoes and the cuffs of his corduroy pants by lifting each foot high before setting it gently down again. Always meticulously neat, six-year-old Little Man never allowed dirt or tears or stains to mar anything he owned. Today was no exception. (Taylor, 1976, pp. 3-4)

Table 2
Progress in Reading for At-Risk (Title I)
Students in Lorraine's Fourth-Grade Classroom

	Fluency-enhanced reading program (2000-2003)	Traditional reading program (1997-2000)
Average instructional reading level at beginning of the year (measured by informal reading inventory)	2.93 grade level	3.00 grade level
Average instructional reading level at end of year (measured by informal reading inventory)	5.80 grade level	4.17 grade level
Percentage of at-risk students exiting fourth grade on or above a fifth-grade level (measured by informal reading inventory)	93%	22%

Note. The silent reading comprehension part of the informal reading inventory was used for the Title I testing. Two different tests were used over the six-year period. An IRI, no longer widely available, was used through May 2001. The Qualitative Reading Inventory–II was used beginning in August 2001. The tests were administered and graded by the Title I staff at our elementary school.

There were nine students in the tested groups during the traditional reading program from 1997 to 2000. These students had a range of second- through fourth-grade silent reading comprehension and were able to read a word list ranging from first- through fourth-grade reading levels.

There were 15 students in the tested groups during the fluency-enhanced reading program from 2000 to 2003. These students had a range of second- through fifth-grade silent-reading comprehension.

students experienced substantial gains in reading rate and oral interpretation of connected text on the Qualitative Reading Inventory–II (1995). The average gain in word recognition (reading word list) was 2.4 years. Over the same period, students gained 48 words correct per minute in rate, nearly doubling what would normally be expected during the fourth-grade year (see Table 2). An even higher gain was found in silent reading comprehension, which went up to 3.2 years (see Table 2). The two Title I students who requested to move out into the partner reading made the greatest gains of the five Title I students. (This observation led to an overall implementation of partner reading among all Title I students the following year, but during our former self-selected reading block.)

The focus on fluency was moving my class toward a reading-centered culture. Students were increasingly involved in book talk on their own time. Instead of my having to implement strategies for children to share books with one another, such sharing became a part of natural talk. Often I heard comments like "Have you read Lemony Snicket yet? I think you would love that since you like Harry Potter so much!"

Parents were also recognizing the impact of this heightened emphasis, telling me touching stories from home. One January afternoon, a parent of a reluctant reader had been working on a work-related project at the computer all day. She had been amazed to see her daughter Sally curled in a chair reading a book for most of the day. Late in the afternoon, Sally piped up, "Mom! We have to get out of here and do something!" Her mom fully expected a suggestion like going shopping or roller-skating. But instead Sally suggested, "How about if we go to [the bookstore] to have hot chocolate while I read and you work?" Sally had learned there was joy in sustained and extended periods of silent reading.

Fluency First: A Three-Pronged Effort in Year 3

After the results of the previous two years of research, I concluded that the three-pronged fluency effort (Readers Theatre, partner reading, and one-minute practice readings) was a worthwhile set of instructional strategies for preparing fourth graders to become lifelong, critically thinking readers (see Figure 3). In 2002–2003, I simply continued the efforts made in the past few years but with some additional modifications.

Readers Theatre

I continued handing out Readers Theatre scripts every Monday morning and having a performance on Friday afternoon. The children continued to love the performances, even though they had begun doing Readers Theatre in earlier grades. The medium did not seem to lose its fascination and challenge.

During 2002–2003 the children wrote and arranged their own scripts more often than before. One of the more intense writing projects was an assignment integrated with North Carolina history. The students were required to create a Readers Theatre script about what really happened to the Lost Colony. The children were assigned to heterogeneous groups and required to write from an assigned point of view: that of John White, the colonists, the Native Americans, or the bears watching behind the trees. This activity probably did more to teach "point of view" than all of the testing strategies upon which I formerly depended. In addition, the activity truly integrated the teaching of communication skills and social studies.

Fridays also found children reading monologues found in first-person text like the first few pages of *Because of Winn-Dixie* (DiCamillo, 2001) or in speeches from favorite movies such as the Gollum monologue in *Lord of the Rings: The Two Towers* (Weinstein, Weinstein, & Zaentz, 2002). Children began to read poetry independently as performers on a stool. By the end of the third year, they were begging me to allow them to choose their own performance materials. There was no argument from me.

Partner Reading

I developed a more organized plan for partner reading with the children. Instead of having the partner reading during the 30-minute Title I block, I scheduled it during self-selected reading. This block in the past had been plagued with

---

Figure 3
An Outline of Fluency Implementation

Year 1: Focused only on Readers Theatre implementation
Handed out scripts on Monday mornings.
• Assigned nightly at-home rehearsals of scripts.
• Performed Readers Theatre on Friday afternoons.

Year 2: Focused on Readers Theatre and timed reads
• Continued the Readers Theatre routine of Friday performances.
• Added timed reads intensely in October and throughout the year in conjunction with writer's craft.
• Implemented partner reading for students not involved in Title I.

Year 3: Focused on Readers Theatre, timed reads, and partner reading
• Continued the Readers Theatre routine of Friday performances, but added student-generated options with monologues and poetry.
• Began a formal partner reading plan with all students during the self-selected reading block, making the transition to independent silent reading during the second semester.
• Used timed reads intensely for one month (January) and throughout the year in conjunction with writer's craft.

"fake readers," students who pretended to read but did not.

I was bothered by the idea that children were wasting this sacred set-aside reading time, so I decided to interview each child in my classroom at the beginning of the school year. I asked a simple question. "In earlier grades, when your teacher gave you self-selected reading time, did you usually read or did you often fake it?" The students' reactions were varied, after they survived the shock of my asking the question. About a third of the class was horrified to even think that anyone would fake read when given the opportunity to read. But these students were the more accomplished readers. The other two thirds were much more verbal about their "faking it" techniques now that they had the permission to share their creative secret practices. And they were indeed very creative. Here are several of their responses.

I wanted to read as fast as my friend, so I watched her as she read. I only read the bottom line of each page and turned the page when she did. But she made 100% on her Accelerated Reader tests and I only made 20%. Joanne

I only read the third paragraph of each page. My teacher was always at her desk grading papers, so it didn't really matter. Jackie

I started at the top, skipped a "hunk," and then read the bottom. Annie

I lifted up the book in front of my face and looked for "fancy" words. Timothy

I looked at the pictures and then told the story by the pictures. George

The greatest puzzle of all was the lowest reader in the class who reported, "I never faked it." I was obviously shocked. Then I prodded a bit. "So you actually read the whole time?" Douglass responded with "I didn't have to fake it at all. I just watched for my teacher to look at me and then I looked down at my book really quick!"

These "fake readers" are the students who need the daily practice of authentic reading the most. It seemed to me that partner reading provided a means to require all students to read and the opportunity for me to observe their reading. So I began the year by pairing up my children so that they could cooperatively learn to actually engage in real reading for an extended period of time and to understand what they had read.

Partners are paired according to interests, reading ability, reading rate, and social compatibility. Although the random assignment of Readers Theatre parts is not connected to a student's reading ability, partner reading is based on reading levels. Because partner reading was substituting for the self-selected reading time, I wanted the children to read on their own with material that challenged them somewhat and required them to collaborate with a partner to negotiate the text and construct meaning (Vygotsky, 1978). I closely supervised the reading time and discussion, and I also acted as a problem solver, but with a twist—the children first had to strive to solve problems with text collaboratively and then call on me only if they needed more aid.

During partner reading, the pairs of children choose reading materials that interest them. They read aloud together for 30 minutes, usually taking turns—one reads and the other follows along tracking the words. They have the choice of how they want to read, whether chorally, taking turns, or reading dialogue in parts. Because I have spent time modeling how to discuss books, the children have learned to monitor and extend their own reading comprehension. When they do not understand a passage, they stop and work as a team to determine what it means. Or they might choose to simply go back to reread. Sometimes, if they are really stumped, they call for me.

One morning during partner reading, two girls called me over. They were reading a nonfiction text they had chosen about sharks. One of the girls reported, "Mrs. Griffith, we have read this sentence over and over again and can't figure out what it means. 'Sharks have long fascinated people.'" I started laughing, immediately imagining a shark with tall people hanging off of its fins who looked fascinated by the experience. We discussed sentence structure and the word *fascinated* being used as a verb in the sentence instead of an adjective to describe the people. Another time, two boys had reread several times a passage in the book *Wringer* (Spinelli, 1998). There was a paragraph followed by numerous lines of unidentified dialogue. They could not tell who was talking. This was a question that I was sure would have been forgotten had they conferred a day or two later on the book. But at the point of confusion I was able to go back into the text with them and help to decipher the two characters who were talking from the preceding paragraph.

In the meantime, I rotated throughout the classroom and conferred with various partners. This has become a wonderful opportunity to eavesdrop on oral reading and ask truly meaningful questions based on the texts students are reading. Here I have a chance to interject those critical thinking questions necessary for test preparation but within the context of their own choice of text. I take notes on children's reading progress and comprehension, noting minilessons that may be needed for a small group or strategies that may need to be retaught.

At the close of the partner reading time, the children make commitments to each other about how many pages they will read in the evening. All of my children are required to read 20 minutes every night. Because the pairs of children have similar reading rates, they come up with an appropriate number of pages to read. Parents have affirmed this accountability system. Children seem to be more serious about reading commitments to a friend than they are to the teacher or a parent. There has been an issue with wanting to read more, and I have a simple solution to that desire—go ahead. But the child has to understand that the partner will be rereading that section the next day during their time together. Rereading is a very profitable activity for children, and I try to always emphasize its value.

One afternoon I asked the children to write some comments about the partner reading plan I had implemented. A number of them commented on friendships that were developing through the pairings. "It shows you how to read whith another kid and it gifs you findes [friends]," wrote one of my lower level readers. "You get to experience other people's expressions and thoughts," wrote

one reader. Another student wrote, "It makes you get to know your friends better."

Other children seemed impressed with the value of book discussions for comprehension. "I understand it a lot better because we talk about the book after every chapter." A lower level reader wrote, "It's fun when you read with people because you can talk to your partner if you don't think that a senises or word dose not make sences." They wrote about learning comprehension techniques from friends: "I learned that if you don't understand it you should read it again. You should talk more about what you're reading." A few of the children wrote that partner reading was distracting to them and that they preferred silent reading. Those students were encouraged to move into silent reading with regular conferences to monitor their comprehension.

Because partner reading is simply a bridge between guided reading and independent silent reading, I encourage children who are reading on grade level to begin silent reading during the partner reading/self-selected reading block in January. All of the children participate in an hour long "silent reading marathon" once a week to develop their ability to read silently for an uninterrupted and sustained period of time.

Writer's Craft/Timed Reads

I continued the use of exemplary passages from award-winning trade books for writer's craft lessons. But I did not time the readings at first. Despite the results from the previous year's exercise in using timed reads to improve reading rate, I consciously decided to downplay reading rate this year, hoping to see the same results using the other methods. I was uncomfortable with some of the techniques I was hearing about from other schools where students were beginning to feel that reading was a race or a hurtful time of comparison to others. Although I had not seen adverse effects in my own classroom, I shied away from the timed reads. I did continue to do one-minute probes each month, and I was surprised this year to see that the progress in reading rate was not happening as steadily as it did the previous year. I have concluded that the ones who are really struggling simply need the push provided by timed reads.

In January, I inserted a month-long emphasis on timed reads again to provide the attention to reading with more energy. Student achievement in this third year has continued the trend that began when I introduced fluency into my reading curriculum.

Third-Year Conclusions

The integration of reading fluency with my reading curriculum has had a dramatic impact on the reading performance of my struggling readers. Gains in fluency and overall reading proficiency were detected among those students (see Table 2). And, although the primary focus of my three-year study has been on those students who qualify for the Title I reading program, I have seen encouraging changes in all of my readers' comprehension as I have focused on fluency. What began as an intervention for at-risk readers has enhanced the performance of all of my children. There are more students at the top end of reading ability interested in dramatic reading and poetry performance. Each year children of all levels in my classroom have become more involved with community theater and church plays. With the shift of focus in fluency from an intervention technique for some to an integral and mediating strategy for all, children seem to be climbing the independent reading levels at breakneck speed. One child at the high end of my 2002–2003 class began the school year at an 8th-grade reading level and finished at a 12th-grade level. The most important change is that our class is passionate about reading, and, because of that, we have come full circle. As children of all reading levels have increased in fluency, their attention to the structure of the text, the development of story, and the deeper meaning of text is made possible. My fourth graders are reading fluently and consequently are thinking meaningfully and critically about text.

Over the course of the past three years I have come to see that reading fluency is indeed an important part of the reading curriculum for all students and especially for those who experience difficulty in reading. I have also learned that reading fluency can be taught in a variety of ways. Teachers interested in making fluency an integral part of their instructional curriculum for reading should rely on certain key principles in designing such instruction: Fluency requires opportunities for students to hear fluent, expressive, and meaningful reading from their teacher, their parents, and their classmates; fluency requires opportunities for students to practice reading texts multiple times; fluency requires opportunities for students to be coached in fluent, expressive, and meaningful reading by their teacher and their classmates; and fluency requires opportunities for students to engage in meaningful and critical discussions of the texts they read and meaningful performances of the texts they practice. How these principles are turned into actual practice depends on the individual teacher. In my own classroom, I found that these principles came to life in Readers Theatre, timed reading, and partner reading and that they had a positive impact on my students' reading development.

Each year there seems to be a miracle story—a child climbs from the bottom to the top rungs of the reading ladder in record time. Taylor was labeled an at-risk student when he entered fourth grade. Still in the lower reading group in April, he had shown only shaky progress from August through November. I hadn't wanted to move him to the higher groups because I felt he still needed the remedial support. But then all of a sudden, as his fluency improved, he jumped to more challenging personal book choices and found he could read much higher leveled books. In April, still in the same lower group of readers, he looked up at me during his Title I group time, and said with a certain level of impertinence, "What am I still doing in *this* reading group, Mrs. Griffith?" He had noticed that he was reading more like the top reading group members. And I wondered how he could have moved up so quickly. It seemed like the skills and the reading fluency had meshed, and he was way above his former peers. While I was working myself into a frenzy teaching these kids to read fluently, he had woken up in the fifth chapter of *The Hobbit* (Tolkien, 1973).

When Taylor was tested, he had moved up to the highest quartile on the state reading test. He had moved from the third-grade silent-reading comprehension level to a junior high level. And his math scores, as measured in word problems, had also risen at a similar rate.

Taylor's goals for the summer? To read The Lord of the Rings trilogy—all three books.

References

Allington, R.L. (1983). Fluency: The neglected goal of the reading program. *The Reading Teacher, 36*, 556–561.

Angelou, M., & Basquiat, J.M. (1998). *Life doesn't frighten me at all*. New York: Stewart, Tabori & Chang.

Braun, W., & Braun, C. (2000a). *Readers Theatre: Scripted rhymes and rhythms*. Winnipeg, MB: Portage & Main Press.

Braun, W., & Braun, C. (2000b). *Readers Theatre: Treasury of stories*. Winnipeg, MB: Portage & Main Press.

Bryan, A. (1989). *Pourquoi tales: The cat's purr, why frog and snake never play together, the fire bringer*. Boston: Houghton Mifflin.

DiCamillo, K. (2001). *Because of Winn-Dixie*. Cambridge, MA: Candlewick Press.

Dixon, N., Davies, A., & Politano, C. (1996). *Learning with Readers Theatre*. Winnipeg, MB: Portage & Main Press.

Fletcher, R., & Portalupi, J. (1998). *Craft lessons: Teaching writing K–8*. Portland, ME: Stenhouse.

Kuhn, M.R., & Stahl, S.A. (2000). *Fluency: A review of developmental and remedial practices*. Ann Arbor, MI: Center for the Improvement of Early Reading Achievement.

LaBerge, D., & Samuels, S.J. (1974). Toward a theory of automatic information processing in reading. *Cognitive Psychology, 6*, 293–323.

Martinez, M., Roser, N., & Strecker, S. (1999). "I never thought I could be a star": A Readers Theatre ticket to reading fluency. *The Reading Teacher, 52*, 326–334.

National Institute of Child Health and Human Development. (2000). *Report of the National Reading Panel. Teaching children to read: An evidence-based assessment of the scientific research literature on reading and its implications for reading instruction* (NIH Publication No. 00-4769). Washington, DC: U.S. Government Printing Office.

Rasinski, T.V. (2000). Speed does matter in reading. *The Reading Teacher, 54*, 146–151.

Rasinski, T.V. (2003). *The fluent reader*. New York: Scholastic.

Rasinski, T.V., & Zutell, J.B. (1996). Is fluency yet a goal of the reading curriculum? In E. Sturtevant & W. Linek (Eds.), *Growing literacy: Yearbook of the College Reading Association* (pp. 237–246). Harrisonburg, VA: College Reading Association.

Ray, K.W. (1999). *Wondrous words*. Urbana, IL: National Council of Teachers of English.

Schreiber, P.A. (1980). On the acquisition of reading fluency. *Journal of Reading Behavior, 12*, 177–186.

Schreiber, P.A. (1987). Prosody and structure in children's syntactic processing. In R. Horowitz & S.J. Samuels (Eds.), *Comprehending oral and written language* (pp. 243–270). New York: Academic Press.

Schreiber, P.A. (1991). Understanding prosody's role in reading acquisition. *Theory Into Practice, 30*, 158–164.

Schreiber, P.A., & Read, C. (1980). Children's use of phonetic cues in spelling, parsing, and—maybe—reading. *Bulletin of the Orton Society, 30*, 209–224.

Spinelli, J. (1998). *Wringer*. New York: HarperTrophy.

Taylor, M. (1976). *Roll of thunder, hear my cry*. New York: Penguin.

Tolkien, J.R.R. (1973). *The hobbit*. Boston: Houghton Mifflin.

Vygotsky, L.S. (1978). *Mind in society: The development of higher psychological processes*. Cambridge, MA: Harvard University Press.

Weinstein, B., Weinstein, H., & Zaentz, S. (Producers). (2002). *Lord of the Rings: The two towers* [Motion picture]. United States: New Line Home Entertainment.

Questions for Reflection

• In the preceding article by Martinez et al., the authors describe ability grouping for Readers Theatre and ensuring that scripts for each performance group were at an appropriate level. In Lorraine Griffith's classroom, the approach was quite consciously not to group by ability. What do you see as the pros and cons of each approach? Which would work better in your classroom? Are there reasons to use both ability and heterogeneous groupings at different times?

• The authors describe Readers Theatre as a way to draw students' attention to writer's craft. Further, in the project's third year, students were involved in writing scripts. In what other ways can Readers Theatre help students make the reading–writing connection?

"I Thought About It All Night": Readers Theatre for Reading Fluency and Motivation

Jo Worthy and Kathryn Prater

Diana: [Reading is] for when we're bored.

Yolanda: Yeah.

Diana: Like when our parents call us from our friends' house.

Yolanda: And it would just be for a few minutes.

Diana: Yeah, when I don't have nothing to do.

That conversation between Yolanda and Diana (pseudonyms) took place in an interview about out-of-school reading attitudes and habits conducted at the beginning of the 2001–2002 school year. The girls' comments are not surprising. Students in the intermediate grades have many things on their minds other than reading. According to Ryan and Patrick (2001), "More so than at any other stage, young adolescents doubt their abilities to succeed at their schoolwork, question the value of doing their schoolwork, and decrease their efforts toward academics" (p. 439). Yet, these years are crucial for developing the independent literacy skills students will need in middle school, high school, and later life.

In our combined 40 years in education, with a recent focus on students with challenges in reading and motivation, we have found one instructional activity that not only combines several effective research-based practices, but also leads to increased engagement with literacy even in very resistant readers. The activity is Readers Theatre, in which students rehearse a poem, joke, story, script, speech, or appropriate text until they can read it with fluency and expression and then perform it for an audience. Readers Theatre differs from other kinds of performances in that participants read rather than memorize their parts. The use of props and physical actions is minimal, and the focus is on how the participants convey meaning through their interpretive reading. Unlike more elaborate performances, Readers Theatre can be a regular instructional activity rather than limited to special occasions. It especially benefits challenged readers, who are rarely given speaking parts in major dramatic productions. With regular reading performances, all students have the opportunity to practice, successfully perform, and increase their self-confidence. Because the level of difficulty of different parts within a script can vary widely, Readers Theatre is an excellent activity for grouping students by interest rather than reading level.

Diana and Yolanda, for example, began participating in Readers Theatre as part of a research study in their classroom that focused on motivational reading materials and instruction. They were both part of a group that performed a script based on Bobbi Salinas's *The Three Little Pigs (Los Tres Cerdos): Nacho, Tito, and Miguel* (1998). As they practiced for the performance

Reprinted from Worthy, J., & Prater, K. (2002). "I thought about it all night": Readers Theatre for reading fluency and motivation. *The Reading Teacher, 56*(3), 294–297.

before their classmates later, Yolanda (as the first pig, Nacho) spontaneously said "I love that part that says, 'No way José, I won't let you in. Not by the hairs on my chinny-chin-chin.'" Diana, who was playing José the wolf, chimed in, "Yeah, yesterday I was going around the house saying, 'Carnitas y chicharrones for supper tonight!' I thought about it all night." The girls' performances were outstanding, and their enthusiasm has carried over into their reading habits. Both now read avidly at home and at school, and the extra practice is evident in their increased reading proficiency.

Anecdotal evidence is important, yet it is also essential that instructional practices be based on sound theory and research. Readers Theatre meets this qualification while effectively addressing the areas of reading fluency, comprehension, and motivation.

Theory and Research Behind Readers Theatre

Fluency is an essential aspect of reading. Children's ability to read fluently does more than make them sound like good readers; it is evidence that they comprehend what they are reading (Dowhower, 1987; Samuels, 1979/1997). The reason for this evidence is still under debate. Does fluent reading lead to improved comprehension? Does good comprehension lead to improved fluency? Although the exact nature of the relationship remains elusive, there is undoubtedly a reciprocal relationship between reading fluency and reading comprehension (Strecker, Roser, & Martinez, 1998). The backbone of Readers Theatre is repeated reading, a tested and proven method for increasing reading fluency in short-term studies, (see review in the National Reading Panel report, 2000). However, the most common types of oral-fluency instruction employing repeated reading target only rate and accuracy. While research studies have documented the effectiveness of these components (Dowhower, 1987; Samuels, 1979/1997), there is a danger that these narrow focuses might give students the impression that reading is about "saying all the words right" and reading quickly. Students need to understand that the goal of all reading is constructing meaning, and it is important that instructional activities have a clear purpose that matches students' needs and interests. Repeated reading, while clearly effective in the short term, may not hold students' attention over long periods.

Readers Theatre, as well as other kinds of reading performance, gives students an authentic reason to engage in repeated reading of texts (Rinehart, 1999; Tyler & Chard, 2000). It is an inherently meaningful, purposeful vehicle for repeated reading. Effective performances are built upon positive social interactions focused on reading, in which modeling, instruction, and feedback are natural components of rehearsals. Even resistant readers eagerly practice for a Readers Theatre performance, reading and rereading scripts numerous times. Reading performance encourages students to read at an appropriate rate rather than to simply read fast without attending to meaning. When students read and interpret texts regularly and evaluate others' performances, they make progress in all aspects of reading.

Choosing and Writing Texts for Performance

There are many ways of "doing" readers' performance or Readers Theatre, and all kinds of material can be used. Many teachers start with books or websites devoted to Readers Theatre but soon find that they need to supplement what is currently available by writing their own scripts. Most scripts are based on fictional picture or chapter books. According to Martinez, Roser, and Strecker (1998/1999), texts chosen for performance should not be above readers' instructional levels. They should have straightforward plots that present characters working through dilemmas requiring talk. It is also helpful to use books from a series or by the same author to capitalize on familiar plot structures, language, and characters (e.g., books in the Fox series by Edward Marshall). Picture book versions of folk and fairy tales are also excellent sources for writing scripts. We have used traditional fairy tales (e.g., Galdone's *The Three Billy Goats Gruff*, 1981), variants of the Cinderella story (e.g., San Souci's *Cendrillon*, 2001), and "fractured" fairy tales (e.g., Scieszka's *The Stinky Cheese Man and Other Fairly Stupid Tales*, 1992; Ross's *The Boy Who Cried Wolf*, 1991). Some books, such as *Hey, Little Ant* (Hoose & Hoose, 1998) are already written in script form. Scenes or excerpts from chapter books and novels (e.g., Ryan's *Esperanza Rising*, 2000; Park's *Junie B. Jones Loves Handsome Warren*, 1996) provide ways to introduce books or follow up with interpretive activities.

Poetry and famous speeches also provide formats for performance and meaningful contexts in which to focus on fluency. Both lend themselves to rhythmic choral reading as well as to independent and group performance. Writing scripts based on information books may seem difficult at first because expository text does not immediately seem adaptable to performance. However, books and poetry related to content area topics in science, history, and math are excellent for improving fluency as well as for supporting conceptual knowledge. In a personal communication, a colleague told me that Christopher Maynard's *Micro Monsters: Life Under the Microscope* (1999) was one of the most popular scripts in her collection. In one performance, several students in her class played the "roles" of mites, lice, and other microscopic insects, describing them in gory but accurate detail while the audience struggled to keep from turning green.

Paul Fleischman's book of poetry about insects, *Joyful Noise: Poems for Two Voices* (1988), is tailor-made for reading performance, as are well-known speeches. With initial support from the teacher, students can and should write their own scripts for Readers Theatre. They can use song lyrics, raps, and poetry for performance. We have found that student scripts are often more creative than teacher scripts. In our classes, we have seen an advertisement for *Freckle Juice* (Blume, 1978), a series of short scenes from the Junie B. Jones books, and transformations of poems by Judith Viorst and Shel Silverstein, all written entirely by students.

Preparing for Performances

It is important that students practice until they can read their parts fluently. Ample rehearsal time makes the difference for struggling readers in any kind of performance. Some struggling readers or reserved students may not want to perform in front of a group initially, but most lose their fear with opportunities to practice a script with a teacher, tutor, or friends in a safe atmosphere. Students can plan, practice, and perform new texts as often as every week. It is important to remember that, as in all group and independent work, students and teachers will need time to plan and establish routines and appropriate behavior. It may take several weeks of explaining, role modeling, and guided practice before such activities run smoothly. As students learn what is needed to prepare for a successful performance, they are motivated to work and practice together productively. This allows the teacher to move from group to group, listening and offering instruction and feedback as students practice.

Unexpected Benefits of Readers Theatre

Readers Theatre has made its way into many classrooms in our school district as we have shared the practice with preservice and inservice teachers and their students. Time after time, teachers have reported that it is the single most motivating, effective reading activity they have used. Recently, two teachers shared some further benefits for students.

In one teacher's third-grade class, a child who had never chosen to read in class before without being required to do so, spontaneously went to the bookshelf, chose Eugene Trivizas's (1997) *The Three Little Wolves and the Big Bad Pig* (the book he was performing for Readers Theatre that week), and took it to his desk to read. Several students in that class have reported practicing their Readers Theatre scripts at home with family members. Brothers, sisters, and parents have taken turns reading the various parts, and parents have supported students with their fluency and expression. Parents also helped their children to make simple costumes for upcoming performances.

Another teacher reported that using Readers Theatre with her fifth-grade bilingual students has contributed to the maintenance of their home language. For example, a fluent English reader whose mother expressed great concern because he was "losing his Spanish," participated in an all-Spanish performance of *Estrellita de Oro* (Hayes, Perez, & Perez, 2002). On his first reading he stumbled through the words, embarrassed that, for once, his reading was not among the most fluent in the class. The next day, the boy read his part fluently and expressively after practicing with his teenage sister.

One boy's story is typical of what happens when resistant readers participate in Readers Theatre. That fourth grader, reading more than two years below grade level, put reading at the top of his "not-to-do" list. According to his teacher, he never chose to read on his own; during free-reading time his attention wandered. Despite the teacher's sincere and skillful attempts, the boy remained apathetic about reading. During the spring, the teacher started a unit on Readers Theatre. She predicted that he would not be enthusiastic, not only because of his dislike of reading, but because he was introverted and reserved. Fortunately, she was wrong. The first set of scripts she used were based on Marc Brown's Arthur series (e.g., *Arthur's Birthday*, 1991). The teacher allowed students to choose the script they wanted to perform, and the students negotiated how to choose the parts in their groups. Not surprisingly, the boy chose the part with the fewest lines (two), and the group began preparing for their performance. At the end of the day, he asked if he could take home one of the scripts to read with his cousin. Trying to hide her shock, the teacher handed him several copies to take with him. The next day the boy came to school reading his part perfectly and even with a hint of expression. As the unit progressed, he began to request "the biggest part" and to become his character in the performances. Readers Theatre made an amazing difference in that student's motivation to read on his own, in his comfort level in the classroom, and ultimately in his reading proficiency.

The teacher's only regret was that she had not begun using Readers Theatre sooner.

In addition to references on the effectiveness of Readers Theatre and fluency instruction, we have included a short list of books to get started on your own Readers Theatre library (see Sidebar). For more suggestions on using reading performance in your classroom, see Worthy, Broaddus, and Ivey (2001), and Tomlinson and Lynch-Brown (2001).

References

Dowhower, S.L. (1987). Effects of repeated readings on selected second grade transition readers' fluency and comprehension. Reading Research Quarterly, 22, 389–406.

Martinez, M.G., Roser, N.L., & Strecker, S.K. (1998/1999). "I never thought I could be a star": A Readers Theatre ticket to fluency. The Reading Teacher, 52, 326–334.

National Reading Panel. (2000). Teaching children to read: An evidence-based assessment of scientific research literature on reading and its implications for reading instruction. Bethesda, MD: National Institutes of Health.

Rinehart, S.D. (1999). "Don't think for a minute that I'm getting up there": Opportunities for Readers' Theatre in a tutorial for children with reading problems. Journal of Reading Psychology, 20, 71–89.

Ryan, A.M., & Patrick, H. (2001). Peer groups as a context for the socialization of adolescents' motivation, engagement, and achievement in school. Educational Psychologist, 35, 101–111.

Samuels, S.J. (1997). The method of repeated readings. The Reading Teacher, 50, 76–81. (Original work published 1979)

Strecker, S.K., Roser, N.L., & Martinez, M.G. (1998). Toward understanding oral reading fluency. In T. Shanahan & F.V. Rodriguez-Brown (Eds.), National Reading Conference yearbook (pp. 295–310). Chicago: National Reading Conference.

Tomlinson, C., & Lynch-Brown, C. (2001). Essentials of children's literature (4th ed.). New York: Allyn & Bacon.

Tyler, B., & Chard, D.J. (2000). Using Readers Theatre to foster fluency in struggling readers: A twist on the repeated reading strategy. Reading and Writing Quarterly, 16, 163–168.

Worthy, J., & Broaddus, K. (2001/2002). Fluency beyond the primary grades: From group performance to silent, independent reading. The Reading Teacher, 55, 334–343.

Worthy, J., Broaddus, K., & Ivey, G. (2001). Pathways to independence: Reading, writing, and learning in grades 3–8. New York: Guilford.

Readers Theatre Suggestions

Internet

Shepard, Aaron. (1997). *Aaron Shepard's RT page*. Retrieved April 14, 1997, from http://www.aaronshep.com.

Picture books

Brown, Marc. (1991). *Arthur's birthday*. New York: Little, Brown.

Galdone, Paul. (1981). *The three billy goats gruff*. New York: Houghton Mifflin.

Hayes, Joe, Perez, Gloria O., & Perez, Lucia A. (2002). *Estrellita de oro/Little gold star: A Cinderella cuento*. El Paso, TX: Cinco Puntos Press.

Hoose, Phillip, & Hoose, Hannah. (1998). *Hey, little ant*. New York: Tricycle Press.

Marshall, Edward. (1983). *Fox at school*. New York: Puffin.

Minters, Frances. (1994). *Cinder-Elly*. New York: Penguin.

Ross, Tony. (1991). *The boy who cried wolf*. New York: Penguin.

Salinas, Bobbi. (1998). *The three little pigs (Los tres cerdos): Nacho, Tito, and Miguel*. Houston, TX: Piñata.

San Souci, Robert. (2001). *Cendrillon: A Caribbean Cinderella*. New York: Aladdin.

Scieszka, Jon. (1992). *The stinky cheese man and other fairly stupid tales*. New York: Viking.

Trivizas, Eugene. (1997). *The three little wolves and the big bad pig*. New York: Simon & Schuster.

Williams, Linda. (1992). *The little old lady who was not afraid of anything*. New York: Simon & Schuster.

Chapter books

Blume, Judy. (1978). *Freckle juice*. New York: Bantam Doubleday.

Clements, Andrew. (1997). *Frindle*. New York: Simon & Schuster.

Park, Barbara. (1996). *Junie B. Jones loves handsome Warren*. New York: Random House.

Paterson, Katherine. (1997). *Bridge to Terabithia*. New York: HarperCollins.

Ryan, Pam M. (2000). *Esperanza rising*. New York: Scholastic.

Information books and poetry

Fleischman, Paul. (1988). *Joyful noise: Poems for two voices*. New York: Harper & Row.

Florian, Douglas. (2000). *Mammalabilia*. New York: Harcourt.

Maynard, Christopher. (1999). *Micro monsters: Life under the microscope*. New York: Dorling Kindersley.

Pinczes, Elinor J. (1993). *One hundred hungry ants*. Boston: Houghton Mifflin.

Scieszka, Jon. (1995). *Math curse*. New York: Viking.

Questions for Reflection

- The authors stress that using information texts for Readers Theatre benefits content area learning. What can you look for in an information text to determine if it might lend itself to adaptation as a script?

- Research has shown that narratives are by far the most commonly found texts in elementary classrooms. If you teach at the elementary level, take a look at your classroom library. Do you have sufficient information texts, including works that could lend themselves to Readers Theatre? If you work at the middle or secondary grades, how can you partner with colleagues in different disciplines to implement Readers Theatre across the curriculum?

Building Fluency, Word-Recognition Ability, and Confidence in Struggling Readers: The Poetry Academy

Lori G. Wilfong

In the fall of 2004, the principal at the elementary school where I worked as a literacy coach asked me to do a reading curriculum-based measurement (CBM) of the third grade. He chose the third grade because those students would be involved in two rounds of state-mandated achievement testing, and he wanted another measure of student progress to identify which students might need extra intervention. A CBM is performed to find out the reading rate and word-recognition abilities of a student (Kuhn & Stahl, 2003; Pink & Leibert, 1986; Rasinski, 2000).

I decided to add a retelling to my CBM. After students read a grade-level passage in a normal manner, I asked them to retell the story to me. I used a rubric to rate them on the number of events they were able to recall (Padak & Rasinski, 2005). I felt that with the combination of words read correctly per minute (WCPM), percentage of words read correctly, and retelling score, I would have a rounded picture of the students' reading abilities. I was able to compare the WCPM score to U.S. norms to see where our students fell in comparison with their age-mates (Hasbrouck & Tindal, 1992).

When looking at the data from the fluency assessment performed in September, I found that almost half of all the students assessed ($N = 86$) were significantly below (20% or more) their grade level in WCPM. In the fall of third grade,

at the 50th percentile, students read an average of 65 WCPM. My own concerns as an advocate for sound literacy instruction surfaced here. As an advocate, I saw a problem that needed to be fixed, and I was set on fixing it. I knew that if I merely reported my findings, it was probable that the 36 students I had identified as significantly below the U.S. norm would be put into a pull-out group for intervention. These groups often receive watered-down reading instruction and are less engaged with text (Allington, 2002; Guthrie, Wigfield, Metsala, & Cox, 2004).

I decided to give my findings to the principal with an intervention of my own ready to be put in place. This is when the Poetry Academy was born. Through my work as a graduate assistant for Nancy Padak and Timothy Rasinski, professors of literacy education at Kent State University, I had read and heard about their research on a program called Fast Start (Padak & Rasinski, 2005). In this program, preschool and primary students read poetry with their parents using a strategy called repeated readings. In this strategy, a piece of text is read and reread to help build fluency, confidence, and comprehension in students (Kuhn & Stahl, 2003; Samuels, 1979). I hypothesized that a similar program would work well with the third graders at Colina Elementary School (CES; pseudonym). The Poetry Academy name came to me as I was reading the fifth book in the Harry Potter series. Hogwarts Academy,

Reprinted from Wilfong, L.G. (2008). Building fluency, word-recognition ability, and confidence in struggling readers: The Poetry Academy. *The Reading Teacher, 62*(1), 4–13.

the school featured in the Harry Potter books, sounds dignified, and I wanted the students who were placed in the Poetry Academy to feel proud of what they were doing. Any student can just read poetry with a volunteer—only *apprentices* got to be in the Poetry Academy.

In this article, the Poetry Academy is described along with the mixed methods research study that was carried out to validate its use as a literacy intervention.

Specifics of the Program

Several factors were influential in the creation of the Poetry Academy. CES already had reading interventions such as tutors and Title I reading in place. Both of these interventions involved pulling the students out of the classroom, so I decided that any new interventions had to be quick and involve minimal pullout from class.

Other researchers such as Moyer (1982) worried that repeated readings may seem like a punishment or boring for older readers. This is why the use of poetry was ideal for its comparatively short text, fun subject matter, and easy match with the strategy of repeated readings (Homan, Klesius, & Hite, 1993; Moyer, 1982; Rasinski, 2000). Mastery of a short poem would cause students to feel confident and successful early in the program, similar to the success that other researchers found in the use of short texts in conjunction with fluency development (Rasinski, Padak, Linek, & Sturtevant, 1994).

The next factor examined was staffing. Like many schools across the nation, CES faces budget constraints. The tutors, Title I teacher, and I, the literacy coach, already had overextended schedules and were unable to find time for any extra help around the school. When I voiced this staffing concern to the principal, he suggested speaking with the community literacy program coordinator. The community literacy program coordinator was happy to give the names of five community members who had time to give. She also volunteered herself for the program, excited to participate in something new.

Components of repeated reading, listening-while-reading, assisted reading, and modeling were all equally important factors in the Poetry Academy process. These components were combined to combat the boredom often associated with repeated reading as a single intervention (Moyer, 1982), to take advantage of the ease of implementation and success of listening-while-reading (Lionetti & Cole, 2004), to take advantage of the one-on-one nature of assisted reading (Hoskisson & Krohm, 1974; Kuhn & Stahl, 2003), and to provide modeling of good reading (Chard, Vaughn, & Tyler, 2002).

Community volunteers attended a two-hour training during which I went over the basics of repeated reading, listening-while-reading, modeling, and assisted reading. I then talked about the program: Each volunteer would be assigned six students identified as disfluent by the CBM and would meet with each student once a week for 5–10 minutes. During this session, the volunteer would introduce to the student a new poem—chosen by me, based on my knowledge of the student's current reading level. The volunteer would begin by reading the poem aloud to the student (modeling) and would then invite the student to read the poem with him or her simultaneously (listening-while-reading, assisted reading). Next, the volunteer would invite the student to read the poem aloud independently (repeated reading) and would provide assistance and praise. At the end of the session, the volunteer and student would discuss what the poem meant to the student, dissect any unknown words, and sometimes just chat about events in the student's life.

The student would take the poem home and read it aloud to as many people as possible, gathering signatures from listeners to verify the reading. The following week's session would start with the student reading the poem one more time to the volunteer to demonstrate mastery of the poem. The volunteer would then introduce another poem, and the cycle would repeat. Figure 1 demonstrates the Poetry Academy cycle.

A few incentives were in place in the Poetry Academy program. I had issued students a folder in which to keep their accumulating poetry and to protect the poems from the ravages of their backpacks. Students often needed reminders to

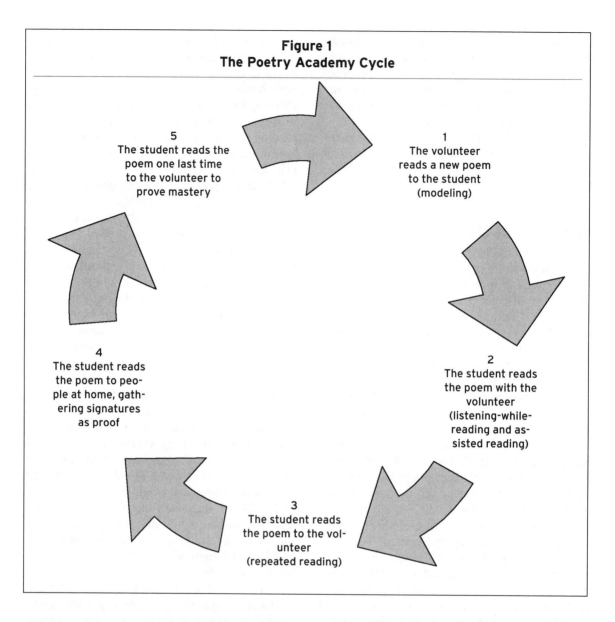

Figure 1
The Poetry Academy Cycle

5
The student reads the poem one last time to the volunteer to prove mastery

1
The volunteer reads a new poem to the student (modeling)

2
The student reads the poem with the volunteer (listening-while-reading and assisted reading)

3
The student reads the poem to the volunteer (repeated reading)

4
The student reads the poem to people at home, gathering signatures as proof

take these home and bring them back for their Poetry Academy sessions, so the volunteers began giving stickers and small pieces of candy to the students who remembered. The other incentive offered to the students was the promise of a Poetry Café to take place at the end of the school year, provided that they participated in the Poetry Academy to the best of their capabilities. The students' parents were invited to take part in a poetry celebration where students selected their favorite poem from the year and performed it in front of the group. We enjoyed pizza, cake, and poetry as each student proudly read his or her poem at an outside pavilion at CES. At the end of the celebration, the apprentices received a certificate commemorating their apprenticeship signed by their volunteer and me.

As stated earlier, I turned to poetry for this intervention because its brief format was ideal for the short sessions with the volunteers. Perfect (2005) pointed out how poetry's format "is especially suited to struggling or reluctant readers, and enhances reading motivation" (p. 17).

When selecting poetry, I turned to the crude, rude, and funny. I wanted students to enjoy their time with their volunteer. I noticed that in my own time in the classroom, humorous text drew students in and held their attention. A plethora of humorous poetry abounds, and I made good use of poems such as "Examination" by Shel Silverstein, from his collection *Where the Sidewalk Ends*; "My Sister Think She's Santa Claus" by Kenn Nesbitt, from his collection *Santa Got Stuck in the Chimney*; "A Bad Case of the Sneezes" by Bruce Lansky, from his collection *If Pigs Could Fly*; and "The Dog Ate My Homework" by Sara Holbrook, from her collection of the same name. I did not perform any type of grade-level identifier when choosing poetry; instead, I considered vocabulary, length, and topic. Each week, I placed copies of two poems in the volunteers' folders. One poem was slightly more difficult than the other to accommodate all of our learners.

Research Takes Shape

Five weeks into the Poetry Academy program, the principal asked me to retest all of the students in the third grade on a different passage on the CBM. The growth that the apprentices in the Poetry Academy were making in comparison with the other students in the third grade was enough to make me and the third-grade teachers take notice. It was then that the research on the Poetry Academy began to take place. The six community volunteers had already been keeping informal data on a volunteer log for me to review, and I was keeping weekly notes on comments made to me by parents, school personnel, and students about the nature of the program. This informal information twisted itself into a sequential-explanatory mixed methods study.

For the purpose of evaluating the Poetry Academy, the participant-oriented approach to program evaluation made the most sense. In this approach, the stakeholders are central in determining the values, criteria, needs, and data for evaluation. Stakeholders are defined as the individuals or groups who have a direct interest in and may be affected by the program being evaluated (Worthen, Sanders, & Fitzpatrick, 1997). The vested stakeholders in the Poetry Academy were the students, their teachers, their parents, the community volunteers, and me. When it became apparent in January 2005 that we were on to something with the 36 students who were involved in the Poetry Academy, I met with these stakeholders to determine the values, criteria, needs, and data to use to evaluate the program. What we decided is as follows:

- Values—The goal of the Poetry Academy is to not only increase fluency, as measured on a CBM by WCPM, word recognition, and a retelling score, but to affect students' attitudes and motivations through reading, as measured on the Elementary Reading Attitude Survey (ERAS; McKenna & Kear, 1990) both before and after the intervention.

- Criteria—Changes in fluency would be measured in comparison with the students not receiving the Poetry Academy intervention (the control group). Fluency scores would also be compared with U.S. fluency norms.

- Needs—More than just statistical numbers must be used to evaluate this program. The voices of students, parents, and teachers must be heard to judge whether this program is a success.

- Data—Data would be collected numerically (fluency scores, attitude scale scores, changes on achievement tests) and narratively (interviews, volunteer logs, focus groups, e-mail).

By bringing stakeholders into the evaluation process, I was able to create a study with results that would be tangible not just to me as a researcher but to the individuals who experienced and helped run the Poetry Academy. This was important to me and to the school and community that I served.

Table 1
Student Participants in the Poetry Academy

	n	Boys n	Girls n	Words correct per minute
Treatment group	36	24	12	x < 65
Control group	50	23	27	x > 65

Table 2
Narrative Data Collection Participants

Participants	n	Type of data
Students	10	Paired interviews
Community volunteers	6	Individual interviews
Teachers	4	Group interview
Parents/guardians	24	Written communication
Other (faculty)	6	Written communication

Participants

The participants in the Poetry Academy were 86 third graders divided into four classrooms at CES, located in a small, rural town in the Midwest. Table 1 describes the student participants in the Poetry Academy. The WCPM on a September CBM for each student was used to separate students into the treatment and control groups: Students who scored below 65 WCPM (or 20% below the U.S. national average of 76 WCPM) were purposively selected for the treatment group.

To gather narrative data about the Poetry Academy, interviews, focus groups, and written communication took place with the various stakeholders. Table 2 details these other participants.

Data Collection

To study the effects of the Poetry Academy, a quasi-experimental, pretest–posttest experimental design was used. This design was chosen for several reasons. The first fluency test conducted in September identified two separate groups: 36 disfluent readers and 50 fluent readers. The Poetry Academy intervention was designed for the disfluent readers, and the 50 additional third graders served as the control group. The intervention was used only with the disfluent readers, because "for students identified as remedial readers, assisted reading was effective in promoting fluency and comprehension development. However, these gains did not generalize to students who were already fluent readers" (Kuhn & Stahl, 2003, p. 13).

The Poetry Academy was scheduled during independent work in language arts instruction in the classroom. During this time, the Poetry Academy students were not exposed to more instruction, a time factor that could have confounded results. Instead, both the treatment and the control groups received equal amounts of language arts instruction. To control for the effects of the Poetry Academy, the treatment group was not pulled out for any additional intervention during the 11 weeks the program took place, including Title I tutoring.

As mentioned earlier, the quantitative data for this study was collected through the use of a CBM using passages at a third-grade level from a commercially prepared informal reading inventory (Burns & Roe, 1992) and the ERAS (McKenna & Kear, 1990). The types of quantitative data collected were as follows:

Curriculum-Based Measurement
• WCPM
• Percentage of word recognition
• Comprehension (via retell)

Elementary Reading Attitude Survey
• Attitude toward academic reading
• Attitude toward recreational reading

Pretest data was collected before the introduction of the Poetry Academy. Posttest data was collected when the Poetry Academy was over.

Qualitative data collection and analysis took place at the end of the Poetry Academy program. As shown in Table 2, group, paired, and individual interviews and written communication formed the basis of narrative data used to evaluate the Poetry Academy. The final qualitative data collection came through my role as a participant observer of the entire Poetry Academy process from inception to implementation to evaluation. Johnson, Avenarius, and Weatherford (2006) described participant observers as a window and a hand in the research process. Not only do participant observers describe what is going on, but they are also able to participate and affect change. I had many chance encounters with the volunteers, students, teachers, administration, and others during the year that the Poetry Academy was implemented. I documented these encounters in research memos and believe they provided great insight on the program (Maxwell, 2005). These served as a guide to all other qualitative data collected to help evaluate the Poetry Academy.

Results and Discussion

Curriculum-Based Measurement

Students in the Poetry Academy made gains greater than those in the control group on the CBM administered before and after the implementation of the program. Statistically significant gains of the treatment group were made in the area of WCPM and word recognition. Tables 3 and 4 show the differences between the treatment and control groups in these areas from semester one and semester two, when the α level is set at 0.05.

Using the strategies of repeated reading, listening-while-reading, and assisted reading, students in the treatment group were able to make gains of an average of 45.06 words per minute. When looking at the oral reading fluency norms set by Hasbrouck and Tindal (1992), students at the 50th percentile made an average gain of 36 words per minute, similar to the average gain of 37.32 words made by the control group in this study. Repeated reading has been shown to increase WCPM through the use of short, simple texts (Homan et al., 1993; Kuhn & Stahl, 2003; Samuels, 1979; Therrien, 2004). Poetry has also

	Table 3 Comparison of Words Correct per Minute		
Group	Mean–Semester one WCPM	Mean–Semester two WCPM	Gain
Poetry Academy	41.83	86.69	45.06*
Control group	87.7	125.02	37.32

*$p < .05$

Table 4
Comparison of Word Recognition Gains by Group

Group	Designation	Semester one	Semester two
Poetry Academy	Independent	7	21*
	Instructional	9	10*
	Frustration	17	5*
Control group	Independent	30	26
	Instructional	11	15
	Frustration	3	3

*p <.05

been used to boost WCPM with positive results (Rasinski & Padak, 2001).

As seen in Table 4, the difference in change in word recognition accuracy is considered significant when compared with the control group at an α level of 0.05. Students were labeled as "independent" in word recognition if they read 99%–100% of the words correctly, "instructional" if they read 95%–98% of the words correctly, and in "frustration" if they read 94% or less of the words correctly.

Word recognition was one of the calls for research made by Kuhn and Stahl (2003). In their call, they asked for a closer study of changes in word recognition using a true experimental or quasi-experimental design (Kuhn & Stahl, 2003). The feedback given to the Poetry Academy students may have assisted in their word recognition gains.

The final CBM was a rating on a retelling using a rubric that appraised comprehension. As seen in Table 5 students in the treatment group did make gains in their comprehension when compared with the control group, and these gains were marginally statistically significant. An example of this change is shown through the "excellent" ratings given both prior to and after program implementation. In semester one, during the pretest CBM, 3 students in the treatment group were labeled with an "excellent" rating on their retelling compared with 13 students from the control group with an "excellent" rating on their retelling. In semester two, when the CBM was readministered, 26 students from the treatment group scored an "excellent" rating, making them equal to their control group counterparts, who also had 26 students with an "excellent" rating.

The findings of the present study mirror those of Homan et al. (1993), where both the control and treatment groups made gains in terms of comprehension as scored on a retelling when repeated reading was used as an intervention with the treatment group. Similarly, the present study fits into the meta-analysis conducted by Therrien (2004), where the method of repeated reading in conjunction with tutoring by an adult and corrective feedback can have an effect on comprehension.

The innovation in method that helped to create these changes in WCPM, word recognition, and retelling was the use of volunteers as literacy intervention. Community volunteers devoted only 5–10 minutes a week per struggling reader and were able to create progress in each of the areas in each student. Future studies using support staff in a similar role are to needed to expand and replicate this innovation in method.

Elementary Reading Attitude Survey
The ERAS can be broken down into two components: academic and recreational reading.

Table 5
Comparison of Story Retelling Gains by Group

Group	Designation	Semester one	Semester two
Poetry Academy	Excellent	3	26
	Good	17	9
	OK	9	1
	Needs work	7	0
Control group	Excellent	13	26
	Good	22	15
	OK	7	2
	Needs work	2	0

A statistic that was seen as significant was the change in attitude toward academic reading between the semester one and semester two administrations of the ERAS for the Poetry Academy students when compared with the control group.

Quantitatively measured changes in attitude toward reading have been proven in other studies (Alexander & Engin, 1986; Kush & Watkins, 1996; Lazarus & Callahan, 2000; McKenna & Kear, 1990; Roettger, Szymczuk, & Millard, 1979). Using either the ERAS or another calibrated instrument, these studies looked into the differences in attitudes over time. Lazarus and Callahan (2000) used the ERAS in a way that is similar to the present study; it was used to determine group differences, whereas the others tracked changes in student attitude toward reading over time. The present study adds to the literature using the ERAS by tracking change with the use of an intervention against a control group.

Significant change in attitude toward academic reading is important because, historically, struggling readers tend to feel more negatively toward reading in school (McKenna & Kear, 1990). It makes sense that when students are comfortable and feel success in a task, they are more likely to enjoy engaging in it. The Poetry Academy helped readers create that comfort and success toward academic reading.

Qualitative Results

Change in the Poetry Academy students was not only observed through the CBMs and ERAS, but through observations made by the students, their teachers and other faculty members, their parents, and the volunteers.

In the postintervention interview, students mentioned the ways in which the Poetry Academy program changed them. They talked about it helping them in various ways:

- "It helped with my reading."
- "It helped me not be embarrassed to read in front of everybody."
- "It helped me understand more words."
- "It helped with the stuttering."
- "It helps with fluency."
- "It helps you read better."
- "It helps you figure out words."

The teachers mentioned the ways in which the Poetry Academy program changed the students as well. The teachers talked about the transformations they saw in attitude and skills:

- A shy student was described as a "little actor."
- There was a "light" that students had when returning to the class after meeting with their volunteer.

Parents of students participating in the Poetry Academy and other faculty also observed changes in the students. Their observations usually related to specific students:

- Zach's mom mentioned that poetry helped Zach like reading.
- Haley's mom talked about how the short format of the poems helped her feel confidence quickly when reading.

The volunteers observed the following changes in attitude and skills in their tutees:

- Increased WCPM
- Reluctance to return to class
- Improvement in confidence
- Improvement in word-attack skills
- Increase in accuracy
- Improvement in comprehension

Advantages of the Program

A volunteer-based program can effect change only if it is supported by those involved (McDaniel, 2002). By including the voices of those concerned, we are ensuring continued support by making changes based on suggestions they give. Advantages of the program as seen and ranked through qualitative data analysis are as follows:

1. Increase in student skills in terms of fluency (WCPM, word recognition, and comprehension)
2. Improvement in attitude toward reading
3. Increased family involvement
4. Poetry as motivation
5. One-on-one attention

Disadvantages, or ideas for improvement, as seen and ranked through qualitative data analysis are as follows:

1. Space for volunteers to work
2. Program expansion
3. Increase in parent communication
4. More intensive training for volunteers
5. Carefully chosen poetry topics

The stakeholders had great ideas for improving the program. Incorporating their voices in the evaluation of the Poetry Academy ensures that future use of the program will run more smoothly and benefit all involved even more.

The advantages suggested by the various stakeholders form the core of the program. The goal was to improve student skills and attitudes, and this was accomplished through the use of poetry, one-on-one attention, and family involvement.

Implications

The Poetry Academy used poetry for literacy intervention with positive results. Teachers, students, volunteers, and parents mentioned the short format of poetry, combined with its usually humorous text, in conjunction with the improvements of the apprentices in their reading skills and attitudes toward reading. The use of poetry in the classroom can help build student confidence and improve their reading skills and attitudes (Certo, 2004; Homan et al., 1993; Moyer, 1982; Perfect, 2005; Rasinski, 2000; Rasinski et al., 1994).

One-on-one attention is a valuable tool. The teachers and volunteers involved in the Poetry Academy referred again and again to the worth of this aspect of the program. I encourage teachers to find time to meet one-on-one with students and to encourage parents to read one-on-one with their children.

As teachers look to use community volunteers to participate in literacy intervention programs, there are certain elements of the present study that should be factored into decisions. First, it is beneficial to train volunteers in the tasks that they will be doing (Burns, Senesac, & Symington, 2004; Invernizzi, Juel, & Rosemary, 1996/1997; Invernizzi, Rosemary, Juel, & Richards, 1997; McDaniel, 2002; Meier & Invernizzi, 2001; Morris, Shaw, & Perney, 1990; Murad & Topping, 2000; Neuman, 1995; Powell-Smith, Shinn, Stoner, & Good, 2000; Wasik, 1998a, 1998b). Volunteers in this study were appreciative of the directions they were given, and it was suggested that even more training might be beneficial in the future. Volunteers also quickly adapted to the routine that was suggested during the training. Creating simple but fun routines to repeat made the process of literacy intervention a pleasure for the volunteers and their students.

When using community volunteers, it is recommended that a reading specialist be a contact for the volunteers and the teacher (Burns et al., 2004; Invernizzi et al., 1996/1997; Invernizzi et al., 1997; McDaniel, 2002; Meier & Invernizzi, 2001; Morris et al., 1990; Murad & Topping, 2000; Wasik, 1998a, 1998b). Even the former classroom teachers who served as volunteers in the present study would stop in to ask me questions about strategies to use with students.

As a reading specialist, I found it advantageous being a part of this program as well. The insights offered by the volunteers helped me assist the classroom teacher with modifying or accommodating classroom work for the students. Through the reading of the weekly logs and informal chats, I got to know the struggling readers at CES even more than I would have had I been there only in a traditional reading specialist role.

It is advisable to use community volunteers for more than just copying and creating bulletin boards (Rasinski & Fredericks, 1991; Sanacore, 1997). The volunteers in this study were grateful to be used in a constructive manner and worked hard when given a concrete goal.

Teachers implementing this program might wish to take advantage of the new depth the Poetry Academy gives to the lives of their struggling readers. Perhaps reviewing the volunteer logs weekly and informally chatting with the volunteers a couple of times a month will help

bring teachers up on the progress of their students. An example from this study is the little girl who sometimes forgot (or purposefully left at home) her glasses. Her teacher did not realize that she was doing this until the volunteer pointed out the student's reluctance to wear her glasses because she did not like them. It is information like this that would be invaluable to the teacher, but that sometimes only another person can provide.

Finally, the principles of the Poetry Academy can fit into a classroom with ease. At its core, the Poetry Academy is dedicated to bringing humor and pleasure in reading to struggling readers. All students can benefit from fun texts and the intrinsic rewards that result from confident, fluent reading. The extrinsic rewards, like the stickers and the promise of a Poetry Café, can serve as motivators in the classroom to continue to propel students to read fluently.

Final Thoughts

The goal when creating this program was to not follow in the footsteps of traditional literacy intervention. Traditionally, literacy intervention is typified by watered-down instruction and segmenting of text that results in a lack of comprehension and interest (Allington, 2002). Instead, the Poetry Academy sought to enrich student lives with personal attention and engaging text while retaining a research-based premise.

Haley, a student identified by her teacher, volunteer, and parents for improvement in both skills and attitude, made a definitive statement about the Poetry Academy during her interview:

> Mrs. W., it didn't seem like school. I knew the whole time I was reading and learning, but it felt like spending time with a friend. If all school was like this, I wouldn't be so bored. I would like to read more.

Haley read weekly with Mrs. O'Neil, who made this statement: "This has just proven to me what just five minutes of reading with your kid can do."

References

Alexander, D.G., & Engin, A.W. (1986). Dimensions of reading attitudes of primary students. *Educational and Psychological Measurement, 46*(4), 887–901. doi:10.1177/001316448604600409

Allington, R.L. (2002). What I've learned about effective reading instruction from a decade of studying exemplary elementary classroom teachers. *Phi Delta Kappan, 83*(10), 740–748.

Burns, M.K., Senesac, B.V., & Symington, T. (2004). The effectiveness of the HOSTS program in improving the reading achievement of children at-risk for reading failure. *Reading Research and Instruction, 43*(2), 87–104.

Burns, P.C., & Roe, B.D. (1992). *Burns/Roe informal reading inventory: Preprimer through twelfth grade.* Boston: Houghton Mifflin.

Certo, J.L. (2004). Cold plums and the old men in the water: Let children read and write "great" poetry. *The Reading Teacher, 58*(3), 266–271. doi:10.1598/RT.58.3.4

Chard, D.J., Vaughn, S., & Tyler, B. (2002). A synthesis of research on effective interventions for building reading fluency with elementary students with learning disabilities. *Journal of Learning Disabilities, 35*(5), 386–406. doi:10.1177/00222194020350050101

Guthrie, J.T., Wigfield, A., Metsala, J.L., & Cox, K.E. (2004). Motivational and cognitive predictors of text comprehension and reading amount. In R.B. Ruddell & N.J. Unrau (Eds.), *Theoretical models and processes of reading* (5th ed., pp. 929–953). Newark, DE: International Reading Association.

Hasbrouck, J.E., & Tindal, G. (1992). Curriculum-based oral reading fluency norms for students in grades 2 through 5. *Teaching Exceptional Children, 24*(3), 41–44.

Homan, S.P., Klesius, J.P., & Hite, C. (1993). Effects of repeated readings and nonrepetitive strategies on students' fluency and comprehension. *The Journal of Educational Research, 87*(2), 94–100.

Hoskisson, K., & Krohm, B. (1974). Reading by immersion: Assisted reading. *Elementary English, 51*(6), 832–836.

Invernizzi, M., Juel, C., & Rosemary, C.A. (1996/1997). A community volunteer tutorial that works. *The Reading Teacher, 50*(4), 304–311.

Invernizzi, M., Rosemary, C.A., Juel, C., & Richards, H.C. (1997). At-risk readers and community volunteers: A 3-year perspective. *Scientific Studies of Reading, 1*(3), 277–300. doi:10.1207/s1532799xssr0103_6

Johnson, J., Avenarius, C., & Weatherford, J. (2006). The active participant-observer: Applying social role analysis to participant observation. *Field Methods, 18*(2), 111–134. doi:10.1177/1525822X05285928

Kuhn, M.R., & Stahl, S.A. (2003). Fluency: A review of developmental and remedial practices. *Journal of Educational Psychology, 95*(1), 3–21. doi:10.1037/0022-0663.95.1.3

Kush, J.C., & Watkins, M.W. (1996). Long-term stability of children's attitudes toward reading. *The Journal of Educational Research, 89*(5), 315–319.

Lazarus, B.D., & Callahan, T. (2000). Attitudes toward reading expressed by elementary school students diagnosed with learning disabilities. *Reading Psychology, 21*(4), 271–282. doi:10.1080/027027100750061921

Lionetti, T.M., & Cole, C.L. (2004). A comparison of the effects of two rates of listening while reading on oral reading fluency and reading comprehension. *Education & Treatment of Children, 27*(2), 114–129.

Maxwell, J. (2005). *Qualitative research design: An interactive approach.* Thousand Oaks, CA: Sage.

McDaniel, D. (2002). Successful implementation of the America Reads program: A case study of an effective partnership. *Reading Improvement, 39*(4), 175–185.

McKenna, M.C., & Kear, D.J. (1990). Measuring attitude toward reading: A new tool for teachers. *The Reading Teacher, 43*(8), 626–639. doi:10.1598/RT.43.8.3

Meier, J.D., & Invernizzi, M. (2001). Book buddies in the Bronx: Testing a model for America Reads. *Journal of Education for Students Placed at Risk, 6*(4), 319–333. doi:10.1207/S15327671ESPR0604_2

Morris, D., Shaw, B., & Perney, J. (1990). Helping low readers in grades 2 and 3: An after-school volunteer tutoring program. *The Elementary School Journal, 91*(2), 132–150. doi:10.1086/461642

Moyer, S.B. (1982). Repeated reading. *Journal of Learning Disabilities, 15*(10), 619–623.

Murad, C.R., & Topping, K.J. (2000). Parents as reading tutors for first graders in Brazil. *School Psychology International, 21*(2), 152–171. doi:10.1177/0143034300212003

Neuman, S.B. (1995). Reading together: A community-supported parent tutoring program. *The Reading Teacher, 49*(2), 120–129.

Padak, N.D., & Rasinski, T.V. (2005). *Fast start for early readers: A research-based, send-home literacy program with 60 reproducible poems and activities that ensures reading success for every child.* New York: Scholastic.

Perfect, K.A. (2005). *Poetry lessons: Everything you need.* New York: Teaching Resources.

Pink, W.T., & Leibert, R.E. (1986). Reading instruction in the elementary school: A proposal for reform. *The Elementary School Journal, 87*(1), 50–67. doi:10.1086/461479

Powell-Smith, K.A., Shinn, M.R., Stoner, G., & Good, R.H. (2000). Parent tutoring in reading using literature and curriculum materials: Impact on student reading achievement. *School Psychology Review, 29*(1), 5–27.

Rasinski, T.V. (2000). Speed does matter in reading. *The Reading Teacher, 54*(2), 146–151.

Rasinski, T.V., & Fredericks, A.D. (1991). Beyond parents and into the community. *The Reading Teacher, 44*(9), 698–700.

Rasinski, T.V., & Padak, N.D. (2001). *From phonics to fluency: Effective teaching of decoding and reading fluency in the elementary school.* New York: Longman.

Rasinski, T.V., Padak, N.D., Linek, W., & Sturtevant, B. (1994). Effects of fluency development on urban second-grade readers. *The Journal of Educational Research, 87*(3), 158–165.

Roettger, D., Szymczuk, M., & Millard, J. (1979). Validation of a reading attitude scale for elementary students and an investigation of the relationship between attitude and achievement. *The Journal of Educational Research, 72*(3), 138–143.

Samuels, S.J. (1979). The method of repeated readings. *The Reading Teacher, 32*(4), 403–408.

Sanacore, J. (1997). Reaching out to a diversity of learners: Innovative educators need substantial support. *Journal of Adolescent & Adult Literacy, 41*(3), 224–230.

Therrien, W.J. (2004). Fluency and comprehension gains as a result of repeated reading: A meta-analysis. *Remedial and Special Education, 25*(4), 252–261.

Wasik, B.A. (1998a). Using volunteers as reading tutors: Guidelines for successful practices. *The Reading Teacher, 51*(7), 562–570.

Wasik, B.A. (1998b). Volunteer tutoring programs in reading: A review. *Reading Research Quarterly, 33*(3), 266–292. doi:10.1598/RRQ.33.3.2

Worthen, B.R., Sanders, J.R., & Fitzpatrick, J.L. (1997). *Program evaluation: Alternative approaches and practical guidelines.* New York: Longman.

Questions for Reflection

- Poetry is sometimes viewed as a difficult genre, and some teachers lack confidence in teaching with it. How comfortable are you with poetry? How can you increase your confidence about using poetry in your classroom? What are some successful strategies that you already employ in your classroom that use poetry?

- Do you agree with the author about the advantages of using poetry with struggling learners? How can you use poetry to benefit not only struggling learners but *all* students in your class?

- The author describes involving all stakeholders—including the students and the volunteers—in determining how best to evaluate the Poetry Academy's success. What do you think of this approach? How often do you involve all stakeholders and participants in similar ways? What might be the advantages or challenges of doing so?

Scaffolded Silent Reading:
A Complement to Guided Repeated
Oral Reading That Works!

D. Ray Reutzel, Cindy D. Jones, Parker C. Fawson, and John A. Smith

Mrs. Taverski (all names used are pseudonyms) had used Sustained Silent Reading or SSR with her third-grade students as a regular part of a daily reading instructional routine for many years. She and other teachers at Green Valley Elementary School firmly believed that students need daily reading practice to become successful, motivated readers.

The school principal, Mrs. Clapton, informed teachers that because the National Reading Panel (NRP; National Institute of Child Health and Human Development [NICHD], 2000) had not found sufficient evidence to support the continued use of SSR, teachers were to stop using SSR and instead have students practice reading by using guided oral repeated readings with feedback. Mrs. Taverski complied with the instructions she was given by her school principal but harbored concerns about when and how her students would be helped to convert their oral reading skills to silent reading, especially in the third grade where many of her students were more than ready to read silently rather than orally.

Mrs. Taverski and other concerned colleagues informally spoke with a university literacy researcher and teacher educator they knew well and trusted. Together the group began a journey that led to a redesign of traditionally implemented SSR called Scaffolded Silent Reading (ScSR).

Perhaps no other single conclusion drawn by the NRP (NICHD, 2000) has sparked more controversy than the lack of research support for time spent reading and the related, prevalent classroom practice of SSR (Allington, 2002; Coles, 2000; Cunningham, 2001; Edmondson & Shannon, 2002; Krashen, 2002). Traditionally, SSR had been incorporated into the daily reading instructional routines of practically every classroom and school across the United States. Not only was SSR popular with many teachers, but also it was popular with some students (Baumann, Hoffman, Duffy-Hester, & Moon, 2000; Baumann, Hoffman, Moon, & Duffy-Hester, 1998; Manning & Manning, 1984; McCracken, 1971; Pressley, Yokoi, & Rankin, 2000; Robertson, Keating, Shenton, & Roberts, 1996).

Although many correlation studies demonstrate a relationship between encouraging students to read independently and reading achievement (Anderson, Wilson, & Fielding, 1988; NICHD, 2000), the NRP (NICHD, 2000) examined only experimental and quasi-experimental studies of the effects of independent reading on reading achievement and found only 10 such studies. Only 1 of the 10 SSR studies in the NRP analysis involved primary-grade students (Collins, 1980). The remaining 9 SSR studies were focused on the use of SSR in intermediate elementary grades or in secondary school settings. Five studies reported no statistically significant effect for SSR

Reprinted from Reutzel, D.R., Jones, C.D., Fawson, P.C., & Smith, J.A. (2008). Scaffolded Silent Reading: A complement to guided repeated oral reading that works! *The Reading Teacher, 62*(3), 194–207.

on students' reading achievement. Five studies found effects favoring SSR, but magnitude-of-effect estimates were of a "noneducationally" significant size or the results were mixed in terms of effects on outcome assessments, such as word reading, vocabulary gains, or comprehension improvements (NICHD, 2000).

In contrast, Krashen (2002) contended that the NRP had misrepresented or underrepresented the research support for SSR (pp. 112–123). A careful review of Krashen's (2002) "expanded set" of SSR studies reveals inclusion of research in which students received reading *instruction* using children's books as well as yet a larger group of poorly designed SSR studies. Advocates of SSR, or similar practices such as Drop Everything and Read (DEAR), suggest that allocating time for students to engage in extended, self-selected, independent, silent reading practice increases students' reading motivation and engagement when compared with other less motivating practices such as round-robin oral reading or the writing of book reports. Despite these claims made for SSR and other similar practices, there has been long-standing concern that some students may fail to make good use of SSR time (Bryan, Fawson, & Reutzel, 2003; Gambrell, 1978; Lee-Daniels & Murray, 2000; Moore, Jones, & Miller, 1980; Robertson et al., 1996; Stahl, 2004).

SSR Concerns and Criticisms

The controversy surrounding traditionally implemented SSR continues unabated to the present time as evidenced by an exchange in *Reading Today* (Krashen, 2006; Shanahan, 2006; Shaw, 2006). Stahl (2004) noted several well-founded concerns and criticisms of traditionally implemented SSR. First, he criticized the conspicuous absence of teacher and student interactions around the reading of texts as a major drawback of SSR. He and others (Worthy & Broadus, 2002) did not recommend the practice where teachers read their own books, presumably as models of reading, during SSR time. He further condemned "the lack of teacher monitoring and accountability for whether or not students are actually

reading during SSR time" (Stahl, 2004, p. 206). Recent research by Bryan et al. (2003) demonstrated that when classroom teachers monitored their students' silent reading during SSR using brief interactions and accountability conferences in which they also provided feedback, even the most disengaged students in the class remained on task for up to three weeks without additional monitoring visits.

As students progress through the grades, the texts they read become longer and more complex. As a consequence, the use of repeated reading of longer texts becomes less and less practical as students develop as readers. Recent research findings demonstrate that even for struggling readers in the second grade, oral wide reading of different texts across genre types rather than repeatedly reading the same text is of equal or greater value in promoting fluency and comprehension development (Kuhn, 2005; Schwanenflugel et al., 2006; Stahl, 2004).

In summary, the implementation of SSR in elementary classrooms has been sharply criticized for a lack of teacher guidance about how students can select appropriately challenging texts to read; poor control of the time allocated for reading practice; little or no teacher interaction with students around reading texts; no feedback to students about the quality and quantity of their reading; and no student accountability, purposes, or goals for the time spent in reading practice. Recent research with disengaged readers during SSR suggests (Stahl, 2004) that teachers ought to forgo the practice of modeling the reading of their own books during SSR and instead monitor students' reading through brief, interactive reading conferences with individual students. Finally, Hiebert (2006) asserted that fluency practice must, at some point, provide opportunities for transferring students' oral reading skills to silent reading.

Where Do We Go From Here?

Some researchers have suggested that instructional scaffolding might improve the effectiveness of SSR, but there have been no studies of the effects of scaffolded silent reading nor descriptions of how this scaffolding of silent reading might be accomplished (Hiebert, 2006). Manning and Manning (1984) have discussed the concept of scaffolding silent reading by giving students a purpose and a definite period of time in which to accomplish the silent reading of a text. Recently, Kelley and Clausen-Grace (2006) offered a "make over" for SSR called R[5] to include five activities—read, relax, reflect, respond, and rap. The authors described one classroom of third-grade students who made gains in comprehension, wide reading, and engagement from using R[5]. Because the report did not specify the group size or compare performance against a control group or a competing treatment, the claimed results for R[5] cannot be clearly interpreted with confidence.

What Is ScSR?

ScSR redesigns silent reading practice conditions to deal affirmatively with past concerns and criticisms surrounding traditionally implemented SSR and puts into practice recommendations by Worthy and Broadus (2002) about moving oral reading fluency to silent reading practice effectively. This redesign was accomplished by incorporating recent findings describing effective elements of reading practice and simultaneously eliminating past ineffective practices associated with traditionally implemented SSR. ScSR is intended to provide students with the necessary support, guidance, structure, accountability, and monitoring so they can transfer their successful oral reading skills to successful and effective silent reading practice.

In traditionally implemented SSR, teachers modeled silent reading and students were provided unguided access to books from home, the school library, or the classroom library. In SSR, students were allowed to choose any book available to them without consideration of difficulty levels. In contrast, in ScSR teachers explicitly teach students book selection strategies so they can select books to read that are at appropriate difficulty levels. Teachers guide students' choices for ScSR by structuring their reading selections to include a wide variety of literary genres.

Ostensibly, the major objective to be achieved in traditionally implemented SSR was to motivate students to engage in reading. Although similar to SSR in this respect, ScSR adds the specific objectives of increasing students' reading fluency and comprehension as well as their engagement with text. In traditionally implemented SSR, teachers did not provide students with feedback nor did they actively monitor their reading practice. In ScSR, teachers monitor students during practice through individual reading conferences in which students read aloud, discuss the book, answer questions, and set goals for completing the reading of the book within a specific time. In SSR, students were not held accountable for reading during allocated reading practice time. In fact, it was often believed that holding students accountable for their time spent in reading practice would negatively affect students' motivation to read. In contrast, in ScSR students were held accountable for reading widely across selected literary genres, setting personal goals for completing the reading of books within a timeframe, conferring with their teacher, and completing response projects to share the books they read with others. The contrasting characteristics of traditionally implemented SSR and ScSR are summarized in Table 1.

To completely understand how ScSR works, we need to step inside an elementary school classroom. To do this, we will observe how Mrs. Taverski implements ScSR in her third-grade classroom.

Putting ScSR Into Practice

Mrs. Taverski, affectionately known as Mrs. T, carefully arranges her classroom library to support and guide her students' book reading choices toward appropriately challenging books. Because students receive less feedback and support in ScSR than in other forms of reading practice, such as oral repeated readings with feedback, Mrs. T has decided that her third graders should practice reading texts they can process accurately and effortlessly (Stahl & Heubach, 2006). She guides her students' book selection by placing reading materials of differing reading

Table 1
Contrasting the Characteristics of Silent Reading Practice in SSR and ScSR

Key characteristics	SSR	ScSR
Teacher instructional role	Model for students silent reading of self-selected books	Teach and scaffold students' appropriate book selection strategies
Classroom library or book collection design	Store and display books in various ways across classroom contexts	Store and display a variety of genres within designated levels of reading difficulty
Characteristics of reading motivation/ engagement	Encourage student free choice of reading materials	Circumscribe student choice to encourage wide reading using a genre selection wheel
Level of text difficulty	Allow students to freely choose the level of difficulty of reading materials	Students are assigned by the teacher to read texts at their independent reading levels
Goal of reading practice	Fostering students' motivation to read	Foster students' motivation to read and reading comprehension and fluency development
Teacher monitoring and feedback	None	Brief 5-minute teacher initiated individual student reading conferences
Student accountability	None	Read aloud to the teacher, answer teacher questions, set personal goals for completing the reading of a book within a timeframe, and complete one or more book response projects

levels on clearly labeled shelves or in plastic bins as shown in Figure 1.

To further assist her students, Mrs. T color-codes the difficulty levels of books within the classroom library collection using cloth tape on the book binding or stickers in the upper right-hand corner of the covers. Mrs. T's students are expected to select and practice reading in books marked by a specific color code representing each student's independent reading level (95% or more accuracy level).

Mrs. T also knows that allowing students the opportunity to choose their reading materials increases their motivation to read (Gambrell, 1996; Guthrie & Wigfield, 1997; Turner & Paris, 1995). On the other hand, she also understands that unguided choice can often lead to students selecting inappropriately difficult books for reading practice (Donovan, Smolkin, & Lomax, 2000; Fresch,

1995). Because recent research suggests that wide reading is effective in promoting students' reading choices as well as fluency and comprehension development (Kelley & Clausen-Grace, 2006; Kuhn, 2005), Mrs. T guides her students to read widely from a variety of literary genres. Students are asked to exercise their right to choose books for reading practice from a reading genre wheel, as shown in Figure 2.

Students in Mrs. T's classroom are expected to read a minimum of five books each nine weeks of the year, across the genres represented in the genre wheel. Once the students have completed reading books representing all of the genres in the reading genre wheel, they begin another genre wheel. They are expected to read enough books each year to complete two reading genre wheels.

Figure 1
Book Storage in Classroom Library by Levels and Genre

Note. Photograph by D. Ray Reutzel.

Having planned the organization, display, and storage of her classroom library, Mrs. T begins her implementation of ScSR by planning and teaching a series of explicit book selection strategy lessons (Reutzel & Fawson, 2002). These lessons are based upon several book selection strategies including the following:

- Orienting students to the classroom library
- Book talks and getting students excited about books
- Selecting a book in the classroom library
- Selecting a "just right" or appropriately leveled book from the classroom library
- Checking the reading level of books

During these book selection strategy lessons students are taught the "three finger" rule. This rule, described by Allington (2006), involves students in marking with the fingers of one hand the words they don't recognize on a page. If there are three or more unrecognized words on a page, the text is considered to be too difficult. Unless students are very interested or motivated by the topic or theme of the book, they should be encouraged to replace the book and select another. An example book selection strategy lesson used in Mrs. T's class is found in Figure 3.

Each day ScSR practice time began with Mrs. T providing a short, 5–8-minute explanation and modeling of an aspect or element of fluent reading or how to use a comprehension strategy using a teacher-selected text. For example, if Mrs. T wanted to focus on helping her students become more expressive through effective phrasing, she provided a lesson on observing the punctuation in the text. She would display a text on the overhead projector. Using marker

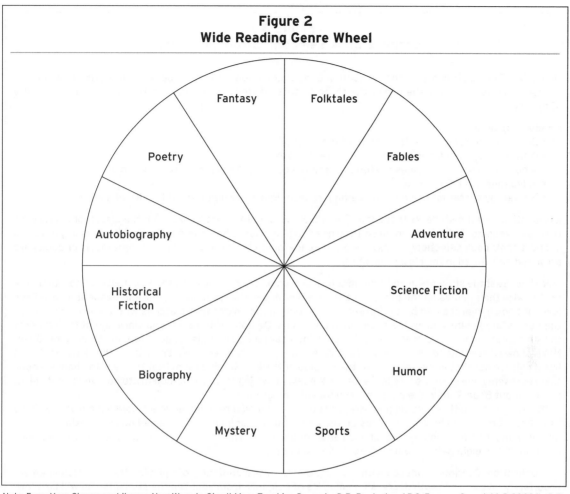

Figure 2
Wide Reading Genre Wheel

Fantasy

Folktales

Poetry

Fables

Autobiography

Adventure

Historical Fiction

Science Fiction

Biography

Humor

Mystery

Sports

Note. From *Your Classroom Library: New Ways to Give It More Teaching Power* by D.R. Reutzel and P.C. Fawson. Copyright © 2002 by D.R. Reutzel and P.C. Fawson. Reprinted by permission of Scholastic Inc.

pens, she color-coded the commas with yellow and the terminal punctuation marks with red. Mrs. T then would model how to use the punctuation marks to phrase the text appropriately. Next, she would also demonstrate how the same text would sound if the punctuation marks were ignored while reading. Finally, she would usually invite the students to join with her in a quick choral reading of the text.

Some days Mrs. T conducts these brief fluency or comprehension lessons on the rug and other days students remain in their seats for these lessons. Following these lessons, students are dismissed to select a new book or retrieve

a previously selected book from the plastic colored bins that contain specific levels of reading materials in Mrs. T's room. Some leveled books are also stored in crates distributed strategically around the room to disperse student traffic flow evenly throughout the room. Students are then free to select a spot in the classroom library, on the carpet, or at their seats for ScSR practice time. During ScSR, the students in Mrs. T's classroom engage in 20 minutes of reading practice time each day.

As students read, Mrs. T retrieves a clipboard from her wall whereon she keeps a listing of students' names for tracking her weekly monitoring teacher–student reading conferences. During each individual conference, Mrs. T asks students to read aloud from their book while she makes a running record analysis of their reading. Recent research has established that an average of three running record analyses within the same level of text difficulty provide a reliable assessment of students' reading progress (Fawson, Ludlow, Reutzel, Sudweeks, & Smith, 2006).

After the student reads aloud for 1–2 minutes, Mrs. T initiates a discussion about the book. To monitor comprehension, Mrs. T usually prompts, "Please tell me about what you just read." Mrs. T usually follows up with general story structure questions if the book is narrative. If the books are about information, Mrs. T asks students to explain the information or answer questions about facts related to the topics. This is a brief discussion of about 2 minutes. Finally, Mrs. T asks her students to set a goal date to finish the book. She also asks the students to think about how they will share what the book is about from a displayed menu of book response projects such as drawing and labeling a "character wanted" poster, making a story map, or filling in a blank graphic organizer.

After each individual reading conference, Mrs. T writes up the student's running record, notes the student's comprehension of the book, records the goal date for book completion, and marks the selected book response project. The form Mrs. T uses to keep student information during these ScSR individual conferences is shown in Figure 4. (A downloadable reproducible of this figure is available at www.reading .org/publications/journals/rt/v62/i3.)

During the allocated 20-minute ScSR session Mrs. T continues individual conferences, meeting with four or five students per day, allowing her to monitor individual students' reading progress weekly. In this way Mrs. T ensures that her students are engaged and accountable for the time spent reading silently, addressing a major criticism of traditionally implemented SSR (Stahl, 2004). At the end of the 20-minute daily ScSR time, students quietly return their books and reading folders containing their genre wheel and personal response projects to their leveled bins in the classroom library or to the storage crates around the room and transition to the next part of the daily routine.

Mrs. T has found that not all of her students are ready to transfer their oral reading skills to silent reading with ScSR. For those students who are not yet ready to be responsible for independent practice, oral repeated reading with a partner continues until behavior indicates an ability to work independently. At this point, Mrs. T starts students on ScSR for continuing their reading practice and transferring their oral reading skill to silent reading practice. But for Mrs. T and other teachers, the question to be answered in the current context is whether or not ScSR is as effective as the type of reading practice recommended by the NRP (NICHD, 2000) called Guided Repeated Oral Reading with feedback (GROR).

How Was ScSR Evaluated?

To determine the effectiveness of ScSR, we conducted a yearlong controlled experiment. The study involved 4 classrooms, 4 third-grade teachers, and 72 third-grade students. Students were randomly assigned to one of two treatment conditions: ScSR with monitoring and wide reading of different genres at students' independent reading levels or GROR of grade-level texts with feedback from teachers and peers. We decided to compare ScSR with GROR rather than SSR for two reasons. First, GROR is the most well-established evidence-based practice to promote reading fluency to which ScSR could be compared (NICHD, 2000). Second, we wanted to explore if ScSR would be an effective means for moving fluent oral reading to silent reading.

To control for teacher effects, all teachers taught both conditions on a rotating basis throughout the year. The schools in which the study was conducted were designated high poverty, low performing schools with approximately 35%–50% African American, Asian, and Latino students, and with over half of the students in the schools qualifying for free or reduced lunch.

Two pre- and two posttest passages (a total of four passages) were drawn from the third-grade Dynamic Indicators of Basic Early Literacy (DIBELS) oral reading fluency (ORF) test: "Pots" and "The Field Trip" (pretest passages), and "My Parents" and "Planting a Garden" (posttest passages). Although there are those who challenge the use of DIBELS for measuring reading fluency (Goodman, 2006), we selected the DIBELS ORF test for two reasons. First, this is a test that is being used in many elementary schools across the United States to assess fluency. Second, the DIBELS ORF test has demonstrated technical adequacy in predictive validity and reliability for measuring students' oral reading fluency (Good & Kaminski, 2002; Rathvon, 2004). One-minute reading samples were scored for accuracy and reading rate (words correct per minute, WCPM). Reading expression in the one-minute samples

Figure 4
Tracking Form for Individual Student Reading Conferences

Student Name _____   Date of Reading Conference _____

Title of Book Student Is Reading _____

Part A: Fluency
Teacher Running Record of Student One-Minute Reading Sample

Number of Words Read _____

Number of Errors _____

Words Read Correctly Per Minute _____

Part B: Comprehension
Student Oral Retelling

Narrative Text:
☐ Setting   ☐ Characters   ☐ Problem   ☐ Goals   ☐ Episode(s)   ☐ Resolution

Expository Text:
☐ Main Idea   ☐ Supporting Detail(s)   ☐ Use of Vocabulary Terms

Questions to Discuss
Narrative: Ask story structure questions about setting, problem, characters, etc.
Expository: Ask about the topic, main idea, supporting details, procedures, explanations, etc.

Part C: Goal Setting
Book Completion Goal Date _____
Goal Pages to Be Read at the Next Reading Conference _____

Part D: Sharing the Book
Book Response Project Selected and Approved With Teacher _____

_____

was evaluated with the Multidimensional Fluency Scale (MFS) using 4 four-point rating subscales: (1) phrasing, (2) smoothness, (3) pacing, and (4) volume. Zutell and Rasinski (1991) report a 0.99 interrater reliability coefficient for the MFS.

Student oral retellings of the 4 third-grade passages were used to assess comprehension and were scored using an idea unit scoring protocol modeled after the Developmental Reading Assessment (Beaver, 1999). Using randomly selected student audiotapes of the oral retellings, two raters used the idea unit oral retelling scoring protocol independently to judge 10 students' oral retellings, yielding a high interrater correlation ($r = 0.94$). The idea units students recalled in oral retellings were proportionally adjusted for the number of words read correctly per minute. A comparison of students' pretest passage mean scores on accuracy, rate, expression, and comprehension confirmed no significant initial differences between the two treatment groups, F (1,70) two passage range F statistics: 0.00–2.80, p range: 0.10–0.99.

Each teacher's fluency instructional time was observed weekly by the school-based literacy coach using a five-item observation rating scale. A random sample of five monthly ratings using the observation scales completed by the district language arts coordinator and a member of the research team revealed a 97% agreement on the ratings of treatment quality and fidelity. All students responded to structured interview questions at the beginning and end of the study. Teachers responded weekly in a Teacher Response Journal (TRJ) and answered a set of structured interview questions at the beginning and end of the study.

How Well Did ScSR Work?

Data were analyzed using analysis of gain scores from the pretest passage to the posttest passage for accuracy, rate, expression, and oral retelling. These analyses demonstrated no significant differences in the pre- to posttest gain scores made between the ScSR or GROR groups at the end of the yearlong experiment on any of the outcome measures of accuracy, rate, or comprehension. The one exception was the ScSR group's gains

in expression for the "My Parents" passage, F $(1, 70) = 8.0, p = 0.006$, which were significantly greater than the GROR group's expression ratings on a single posttest passage.

Figures 5–8 show the average gains made by the ScSR and GROR fluency treatments from the beginning-of-year to end-of-year growth in accuracy, rate, expression and comprehension from the fall to spring of the third-grade year. ScSR and GROR reading practice approaches resulted in a 21% average reduction in the number of reading errors over the course of the yearlong study (see Figure 5), a 27% average increase in the mean number of words read correctly per minute over the course of the study (see Figure 6), and a 20% average increase in expressive reading qualities including phrasing, volume, smoothness, and pacing (see Figure 7).

ScSR and GROR approaches also resulted in a 43% average increase in the proportion of idea units recalled divided by the number of words read correctly per minute over the course of the yearlong study (see Figure 8). Consequently, for all intents and purposes, students in the ScSR experimental group made progress equivalent to students in the scientifically validated comparison reading practice condition of GROR as recommended by the NRP (NICHD, 2000) in reading accuracy, rate, expression, and comprehension. In summary, these findings can be interpreted to indicate that ScSR represents an equivalent, complementary practice to GROR for improving third-grade students' fluency and comprehension.

All students responded to the structured interview questions. Student responses across both comparison groups to structured interview question 1, How do you think your reading aloud sounds?, in the fall were quite brief. Responses ranged from "Not very good" to "OK" to "Kind of good." In the spring of the year, student responses in both comparison groups were also brief but had shifted to "Good" and other similarly positive comments. ScSR student "good" responses had moved from 30% in the fall to 71% in the spring. GROR student "good" responses had moved from 38% in the fall to 59% in the spring.

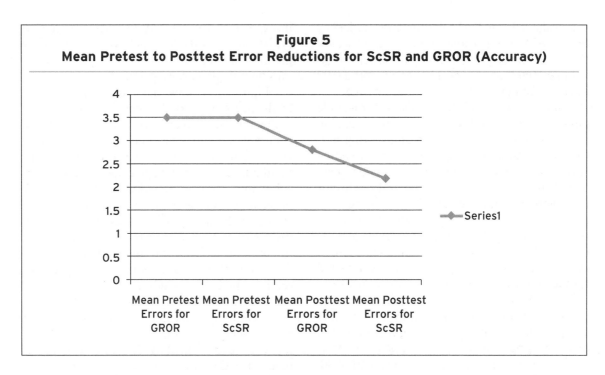

Figure 5
Mean Pretest to Posttest Error Reductions for ScSR and GROR (Accuracy)

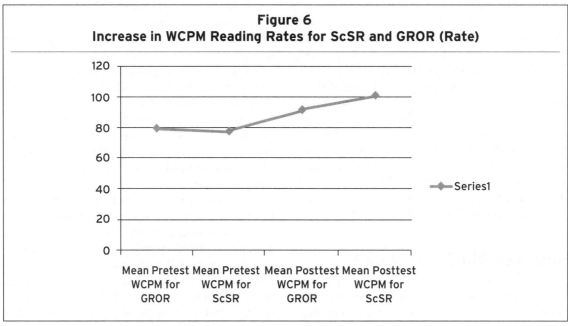

Figure 6
Increase in WCPM Reading Rates for ScSR and GROR (Rate)

Student responses in the ScSR and GROR groups in the fall to structured interview question 2, If you don't think your reading aloud sounds good, what do you do to fix it?, evoked responses such as "read more often," "practice," "read louder," "read it again over and over," "read the words correctly," or "read it over until it sounds right." In the spring, students in both groups had more

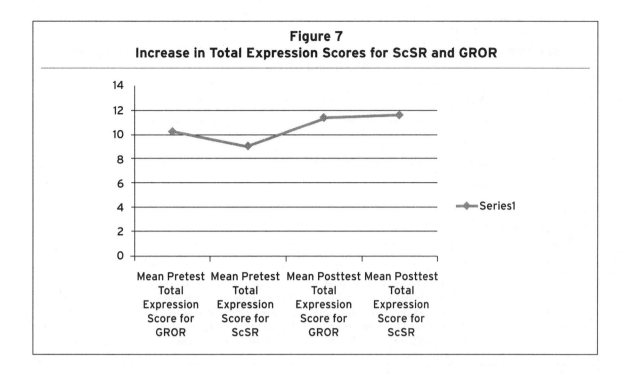

Figure 7
Increase in Total Expression Scores for ScSR and GROR

elaborated responses to this question. Students in the ScSR group responded with "Read more, practice," "Practice silently, then read out loud every day," "Read more, read slower to understand the words, not just go through it quickly," or "Slow reading down, think more, and take a big breath and read to the comma or end punctuation." Students in the GROR group responded with "Read slowly so the person I was reading to could understand," "Take your time with your reading so you get it right," or "Read aloud every day, adjust your reading speed to go slower when the text is hard or new; use expression."

Student responses in the spring to structured interview question 3, What does a good reader sound like to you?, showed similar patterns of elaborated understanding of the concept of good reading. The ScSR and GROR student responses were similar, with students saying that a good reader is "Someone who goes back and fixes mistakes," "Someone who reads smooth, clearly, and loud enough that others can hear," "Someone who read lots of books," "Someone who watches commas and exclamation points," and so on.

Teacher reflections recorded in weekly journal entries about the ScSR practice condition included narrative comments such as "The students who love to read are enjoying this time." "More students are reading chapter books and seem to be really enjoying them." "Kids are really enjoying and getting more expressive in their oral reading." "Some students who did not enjoy reading are now completing their books." One teacher wrote, "I appreciate the quiet time of ScSR. What is wrong with letting students read? I think it is beneficial." Another remarked, "Some students who did not enjoy reading before are completing their books!" In the GROR practice condition one teacher wrote, "The students are reading, practicing, and performing. Rereading has become automatic to some students. I heard one child ask her partner if what they [sic] read made sense. Her partner read the sentence again and they continued." Another teacher stated, "I have noticed the expression of my students is improving. They are stopping and rereading with greater expression."

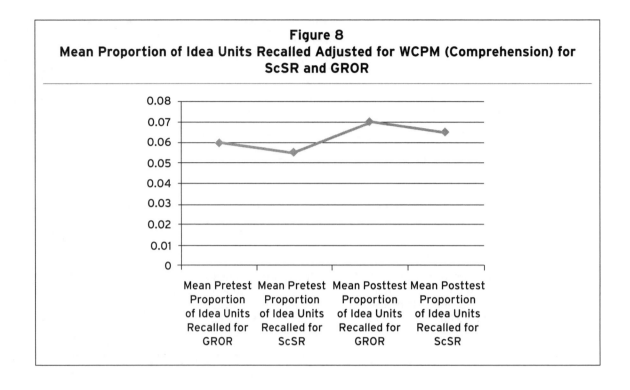

Figure 8
Mean Proportion of Idea Units Recalled Adjusted for WCPM (Comprehension) for ScSR and GROR

Finally, ScSR teacher responses to the structured interview question, What effects, if any, are you noticing on your students with each fluency practice condition?, included initial complaints about student participation during silent reading. One teacher wrote, "I notice now that some students just do not read during the 20 minutes of practice." Another wrote, "Students who really want me to hear them practice are developing good skills. I notice that some students do not like to be heard or perform." Still another teacher reported, "They like to read. I enjoy hearing the students tell me about their reading. The excitement and energy is contagious when they read a book they enjoy!"

What Can We Conclude About the Effectiveness of ScSR?

In this study, the effects of the ScSR treatment were compared with the NRP scientifically validated reading practice approach of GROR. The ScSR reading practice approach was systematically designed to address acknowledged concerns surrounding past implementations of traditional SSR reading practice. Some of these weaknesses included: (a) no teacher guidance about how students can select appropriately challenging texts to read; (b) poor control of the time allocated for reading practice; (c) little or no teacher interaction with students around reading texts; (d) no feedback to students about the quality and quantity of their reading; and (e) no student accountability, purposes, or goals for the time spent in reading practice.

The finding of no significant differences between the two contrasting ScSR and GROR reading practice treatment conditions for improving third-grade students' accuracy, reading rates, expression (with the exception of a single passage favoring ScSR), and comprehension retelling scores, at first seemed disappointing. However, when properly viewed, these findings indicate that the ScSR practice approach was found to be, for all intents and purposes, equal to the effects of the evidence-based approach of GROR—at least with regard to improvements in accuracy, reading rate, expression, and comprehension for this sample of third-grade students.

Our qualitative findings showed that any single reading practice approach used exclusively over long periods of time tends toward tedium for both teachers and students. Thus, ScSR provides third-grade teachers access to an alternative for practicing reading that decreases errors and increases students' reading rates, use of expression, and comprehension.

These findings effectively argue that ScSR—in which teachers guide the selection of texts, encourage wide reading, monitor student progress, discuss books briefly, provide students with feedback, and require accountability for time spent reading silently—represents a viable, complementary, and motivating approach that is comparable to the NRP-recommended reading practice of GROR for this sample of third-grade students.

Mrs. Taverski's third-grade classroom now uses both GROR and ScSR to read, re-read, perform, discuss, and share the joy of becoming increasingly fluent readers. No longer are Mrs. Taverski and her students confined to a single approach for facilitating reading fluency practice. Rather Mrs. Taverski alternates using two effective reading fluency practice approaches with her students that lead to increased motivation, reading fluency, and reading comprehension.

References

Allington, R.L. (Ed.) (2002). *Big brother and the national reading curriculum: How ideology trumped evidence*. Portsmouth, NH: Heinemann.

Allington, R.L. (2006). *What really matters for struggling readers: Designing research-based programs* (2nd ed.). Boston: Allyn & Bacon.

Anderson, R.C., Wilson, P.T., & Fielding, L.G. (1988). Growth in reading and how children spend their time outside of school. *Reading Research Quarterly, 23*(3), 285–303. doi:10.1598/RRQ.23.3.2

Baumann, J.F., Hoffman, J.V., Duffy-Hester, A., & Moon, J.R. (2000). "The first R" yesterday and today: U.S. elementary reading instruction practices reported by teachers and administrators. *Reading Research Quarterly, 35*(3), 338–377. doi:10.1598/RRQ.35.3.2

Baumann, J.F., Hoffman, J.V., Moon, J.R., & Duffy-Hester, A. (1998). Where are teachers' voices in the phonics/whole language debate? Results from a survey of U.S.

elementary classroom teachers. *The Reading Teacher, 51*(8), 636–650.

Beaver, J. (1999). *Developmental reading assessment*. Upper Saddle River, NJ: Scott Foresman.

Bryan, G., Fawson, P.C., & Reutzel, D.R. (2003). Sustained silent reading: Exploring the value of literature discussion with three non-engaged readers. *Reading Research and Instruction, 43*(1), 47–73.

Coles, G. (2000). *Misreading reading: The bad science that hurts children*. Portsmouth, NH: Heinemann.

Collins, C. (1980). Sustained silent reading periods: Effects on teachers' behaviors and students' achievement. *The Elementary School Journal, 81*(2), 108–114. doi:10.1086/461213

Cunningham, J.W. (2001). The National Reading Panel Report. *Reading Research Quarterly, 36*(3), 326–335. doi:10.1598/RRQ.36.3.5

Donovan, C.A., Smolkin, L.B., & Lomax, R.G. (2000). Beyond the independent-level text: Considering the reader-text match in first-graders' self-selections during recreational reading. *Reading Psychology, 21*(4), 309–333.

Edmondson, J., & Shannon, P. (2002). The will of the people. In R.L. Allington (Ed.), *Big brother and the national reading curriculum: How ideology trumped evidence* (pp. 224–231). Portsmouth, NH: Heinemann.

Fawson, P.C., Ludlow, B., Reutzel, D.R., Sudweeks, R., & Smith, J.A. (2006). Examining the reliability of running records: Attaining generalizable results. *The Journal of Educational Research, 100*(2), 113–126. doi:10.3200/JOER.100.2.113-126

Fresch, M.J. (1995). Self-selection of early literacy learners. *The Reading Teacher, 49*(3), 220–227.

Gambrell, L.B. (1978). Getting started with sustained silent reading and keeping it going. *The Reading Teacher, 32*(3), 328–331.

Gambrell, L.B. (1996). Creating classroom cultures that foster reading motivation. *The Reading Teacher, 50*(1), 14–25.

Good, R.H., & Kaminski, R.A. (2002). *DIBELS oral reading fluency passages for first through third grades* (Technical Report No. 10). Eugene: University of Oregon.

Goodman, K.S. (2006). *The truth about DIBELS: What it is, what it does*. Portsmouth, NH: Heinemann.

Guthrie, J.T., & Wigfield, A. (Eds.) (1997). *Reading engagement: Motivating readers through integrated instruction*. Newark, DE: International Reading Association.

Hiebert, E.H. (2006). Becoming fluent: Repeated reading with scaffolded texts. In S.J. Samuels & A.E. Farstrup (Eds.), *What research has to say about fluency instruction* (pp. 204–226). Newark, DE: International Reading Association.

Kelley, M., & Clausen-Grace, N. (2006). R⁵: The sustained silent reading makeover that transformed readers. *The Reading Teacher, 60*(2), 148–157. doi:10.1598/RT.60.2.5

Krashen, S. (2002). More smoke and mirrors: A critique of the National Reading Panel Report on fluency. In R.L.

Allington (Ed.), *Big brother and the national reading curriculum: How ideology trumped evidence* (pp. 112–124). Portsmouth, NH: Heinemann.

Krashen, S. (2006). SSR is a very good idea: A response to Shanahan. *Reading Today, 24*(1), 16.

Kuhn, M.R. (2005). A comparative study of small group fluency instruction. *Reading Psychology, 26*(2), 127–146. doi:10.1080/02702710590930492

Lee-Daniels, S.L., & Murray, B.A. (2000). DEAR me: What does it take to get my students reading? *The Reading Teacher, 54*(2), 154–155.

Manning, G.L., & Manning, M. (1984). What models of recreational reading make a difference? *Reading World, 23*(4), 375–380.

McCracken, R.A. (1971). Initiating sustained silent reading. *Journal of Reading, 14*(8), 521–524, 582–583.

Moore, J.C., Jones, C.J., & Miller, D.C. (1980). What we know after a decade of sustained silent reading. *The Reading Teacher, 33*(4), 445–450.

National Institute of Child Health and Human Development. (2000). *Report of the National Reading Panel. Teaching children to read: An evidence-based assessment of the scientific research literature on reading and its implications for reading instruction* (NIH Publication No. 00-4769). Washington, DC: U.S. Government Printing Office.

Pressley, M., Yokoi, L., & Rankin, J. (2000). A survey of instructional practices of primary teachers nominated as effective in promoting literacy. In R.D. Robinson, M.C. McKenna, & J.M. Wedman (Eds.), *Issues and trends in literacy education* (2nd ed., pp. 10–34). Boston: Allyn & Bacon.

Rathvon, N. (2004). *Early reading assessment: A practitioner's handbook*. New York: Guilford.

Reutzel, D.R., & Fawson, P.C. (2002). *Your classroom library: New ways to give it more teaching power: Great teacher-tested and research-based strategies for organizing and using your library to increase students' reading achievement*. New York: Scholastic.

Robertson, C., Keating, I., Shenton, L., & Roberts, I. (1996). Uninterrupted, sustained, silent reading: The rhetoric and the practice. *Journal of Research in Reading, 19*(1), 25–35. doi:10.1111/j.1467-9817.1996.tb00084.x

Schwanenflugel, P.J., Meisinger, E.B., Wisenbaker, J.M., Kuhn, M.R., Strauss, G.P., & Morris, R.D. (2006). Becoming a fluent and automatic reader in the early elementary school years. *Reading Research Quarterly, 41*(4), 496–523. doi:10.1598/RRQ.41.4.4

Shanahan, T. (2006). Does he really think kids shouldn't read? *Reading Today, 23*(6), 12.

Shaw, M.L. (2006). Sustained silent reading: Another view. *Reading Today, 24*(1), 16.

Stahl, S. (2004). What do we know about fluency? In P. McCardle & V. Chhabra (Eds.), *The voice of evidence in reading research* (pp. 187–211). Baltimore: Paul H. Brookes.

Stahl, S.A., & Heubach, K. (2006). Fluency-oriented reading instruction. In K.A. Dougherty Stahl & M.C. McKenna (Eds.), *Reading research at work: Foundations of effective practice* (pp. 177–204). New York: Guilford.

Turner, J., & Paris, S.G. (1995). How literacy tasks influence children's motivation for literacy. *The Reading Teacher, 48*(8), 662–673.

Worthy, J., & Broadus, K. (2002). Fluency beyond the primary grades: From group performance to silent, independent reading. *The Reading Teacher, 55*(4), 334–343.

Zutell, J., & Rasinski, T.V. (1991). Training teachers to attend to their students' oral reading fluency. *Theory Into Practice, 30*(3), 211–217.

Questions for Reflection

- Do you use some form of sustained silent reading in your classroom? How "tuned in" are you to what students are doing during SSR? How effective has SSR been for your students? How do you know?

- Author Ray Reutzel adds, If you aren't giving your students a chance to read silently, why not? What conditions do you think promote effective silent reading practice? What do teachers think reading silently on their own demonstrates or teaches students about the reading process?

- Scaffolded Silent Reading is described here in a third-grade classroom, and the authors suggest that it is helpful for supporting students as they grow as readers and move from oral to silent reading. How might ScSR benefit students who have already made that transition? For these students, do you believe that ScSR would be of more benefit that SSR? Why or why not?

Oral Reading Fluency Norms:
A Valuable Assessment Tool
for Reading Teachers

Jan Hasbrouck and Gerald A. Tindal

Teachers have long known that having students learn to process written text fluently, with appropriate rate, accuracy, and expression—making reading sound like language (Stahl & Kuhn, 2002)—is important in the overall development of proficient reading. However, the fundamental link between reading fluency and comprehension, especially in students who struggle with reading, may have been new news to some teachers (Pikulski & Chard, 2005). Following the publication of the National Reading Panel report (National Institute of Child Health and Human Development, 2000), many teachers and reading specialists are now focusing significant attention on developing their students' fluency skills.

Curriculum-Based Measurement and Oral Reading Fluency

Educators looking for a way to assess students' reading fluency have at times turned to curriculum-based measurement (CBM). CBM is a set of standardized and well-researched procedures for assessing and monitoring students' progress in reading, math, spelling, and writing (Fuchs & Deno, 1991; Shinn, 1989, 1998; Tindal & Marston, 1990). One widely used CBM procedure is the assessment of oral reading fluency (ORF), which focuses on two of the three components of fluency: rate and accuracy. A teacher listens to a student read aloud from an unpracticed passage for one minute. At the end of the minute each error is subtracted from the total number of words read to calculate the score of words correct per minute (WCPM). For a full description of the standardized CBM procedures for assessing oral reading fluency, see Shinn (1989).

WCPM has been shown, in both theoretical and empirical research, to serve as an accurate and powerful indicator of overall reading competence, especially in its strong correlation with comprehension. The validity and reliability of these two measures have been well established in a body of research extending over the past 25 years (Fuchs, Fuchs, Hosp, & Jenkins, 2001; Shinn, 1998). The relationship between ORF and comprehension has been found to be stronger with elementary and junior high students than with older individuals (Fuchs et al., 2001).

National Norms for Oral Reading Fluency Performance
National ORF Norms: 1992

In 1992 we published an article that contained a table of ORF norms that reported percentile scores for students in grades 2–5 at three times (fall, winter, and spring) for each grade. These performance norms were created by compiling data from eight geographically and

Hasbrouck, J., & Tindal, G.A. (2006). Oral reading fluency norms: A valuable assessment tool for reading teachers. *The Reading Teacher, 59*(7), 636–644.

demographically diverse school districts in the United States. These districts all had used standardized CBM procedures to collect their ORF data. There were several limitations to the original 1992 ORF norms. For example, they contained scores only for grades 2–5. In addition, the data obtained in that original study allowed us to compile norms only for the 75th, 50th, and 25th percentiles.

Time to Revisit National ORF Norms

Over a decade later, the interest in fluency by teachers and administrators has grown tremendously. By 2005, fluency had made it to both the "what's hot" and the "what should be hot" categories of the annual survey of national reading experts to determine current key issues (Cassidy & Cassidy, 2004/2005). Materials designed specifically to help teachers teach reading fluency have been developed such as *Read Naturally* (Ihnot, 1991), *QuickReads* (Hiebert, 2002), and *The Six-Minute Solution* (Adams & Brown, 2003). Publications designed to help teachers understand what fluency is and how to teach it (see Osborn & Lehr, 2004), as well as how to assess reading fluency (see Rasinski, 2004), are now readily available. Articles about reading fluency frequently appear in major professional reading journals, including *The Reading Teacher*. Recent examples are Hudson, Lane, and Pullen (2005); Kuhn (2004/2005); and Pikulski and Chard (2005).

From kindergarten through grade 3 a common practice has been to compare fluency scores with established norms or benchmarks for (a) screening students to determine if an individual student may need targeted reading assistance, and (b) monitoring students' reading progress. Examples of benchmark assessments include DIBELS (Good & Kaminski, 2002), AIMSweb (Edformation, 2004), the Texas Primary Reading Inventory—TPRI (Texas Education Agency, 2004), and the Reading Fluency Monitor (Read Naturally, 2002). With escalating interest in assessing and teaching reading fluency in the past decade, professional educators must be certain

that they have the most current and accurate information available to them.

National ORF Norms: 2005

New national performance norms for oral reading fluency have now been developed. These new ORF norms were created from a far larger number of scores, ranging from a low of 3,496 (in the winter assessment period for eighth graders) to a high of 20,128 scores (in the spring assessment of second graders). We collected data from schools and districts in 23 states and were able to compile more detailed norms, reporting percentiles from the 90th through the 10th percentile levels. To ensure that these new norms represented reasonably current student performance, we used only ORF data collected between the fall of 2000 through the 2004 school year.

All the ORF data used in this current compilation were collected using traditional CBM procedures that mandate that every student in a classroom—or a representative sample of students from all levels of achievement—be assessed. Following these procedures, reading scores were collected from the full range of students, from those identified as gifted or otherwise exceptionally skillful to those diagnosed with reading disabilities such as dyslexia. Students learning to speak English who receive reading instruction in a regular classroom also have been represented in this sample, although the exact proportion of these students is unknown. (A complete summary of the data files used to compile the norms table in this article is available at the website of Behavioral Research & Teaching at the University of Oregon: http://brt.uoregon.edu/techreports/TR_33_NCORF_DescStats.pdf [Behavioral Research and Teaching, 2005].)

Using ORF Norms for Making Key Decisions

Everyone associated with schools today is aware of the increasing requirements for data-driven accountability for student performance. The federal No Child Left Behind (NCLB) Act of 2001 (NCLB, 2002) mandates that U.S. schools demonstrate Adequate Yearly Progress (AYP). In turn, state and local education agencies are requiring schools to demonstrate that individual students are meeting specified benchmarks indicated in state standards. This amplified focus on accountability necessarily requires increased collection of assessment data, in both special and general education settings (Linn, 2000; McLaughlin & Thurlow, 2003).

Four Categories of Reading Assessments

Reading assessments have recently been categorized to match four different decision-making purposes: screening, diagnostic, progress monitoring, and outcome (Kame'enui, 2002).

- *Screening measures*: Brief assessments that focus on critical reading skills that predict future reading growth and development, conducted at the beginning of the school year to identify children likely to need extra or alternative forms of instruction.

- *Diagnostic measures*: Assessments conducted at any time during the school year when a more in-depth analysis of a student's strengths and needs is necessary to guide instructional decisions.

- *Progress-monitoring measures*: Assessments conducted at a minimum of three times a year or on a routine basis (e.g., weekly, monthly, or quarterly) using comparable and multiple test forms to (a) estimate rates of reading improvement, (b) identify students who are not demonstrating adequate progress and may require additional or different forms of instruction, and (c) evaluate the effectiveness of different forms of instruction for struggling readers and provide direction for developing more effective instructional programs for those challenged learners.

- *Outcome measures*: Assessments for the purpose of determining whether students achieved grade-level performance or demonstrated improvement.

The Role of ORF in Reading Assessment

Fuchs et al. (2001) have suggested that ORF assessments can play a role in screening and progress monitoring. Some initial research by Hosp and Fuchs (2005) also provides support for the use of traditional CBM measures as a way of diagnosing difficulties in reading subskills. Having current norms available can help guide teachers in using ORF assessment results to make key instructional decisions for screening, diagnosis, and progress monitoring.

The ORF norms presented in Table 1 provide scores for students in grades 1–8 for three different time periods across a school year. For each grade level, scores are presented for five different percentile rankings: 90th, 75th, 50th, 25th, and 10th. In order to use these norms for making instructional or placement decisions about their own students, teachers must be certain to follow the CBM procedures carefully to collect ORF scores.

ORF Norms for Screening Decisions

Rationale and Support for Screening Reading

Screening measures help a teacher quickly identify which students are likely "on track" to achieve future success in overall reading competence and which ones may need extra assistance. Screening measures are commonly developed from research examining the capacity of an assessment to predict future, complex performance based on a current, simple measure of performance. These assessments are designed to be time efficient to minimize the impact on instructional time. Research has clearly indicated the critical need to provide high-quality, intensive instructional interventions to students at risk for reading difficulty as soon as possible (Snow, Burns, & Griffin, 1998). Increasingly, teachers are being required to administer screening measures to every student, especially those in kindergarten through grade 3, because of the

Table 1
Oral Reading Fluency Norms, Grades 1-8

Grade	Percentile	Fall WCPM	Winter WCPM	Spring WCPM
1	90		81	111
	75		47	82
	50		23	53
	25		12	28
	10		6	15
	SD		32	39
	Count		16,950	19,434
2	90	106	125	142
	75	79	100	117
	50	51	72	89
	25	25	42	61
	10	11	18	31
	SD	37	41	42
	Count	15,896	18,229	20,128
3	90	128	146	162
	75	99	120	137
	50	71	92	107
	25	44	62	78
	10	21	36	48
	SD	40	43	44
	Count	16,988	17,383	18,372
4	90	145	166	180
	75	119	139	152
	50	94	112	123
	25	68	87	98
	10	45	61	72
	SD	40	41	43
	Count	16,523	14,572	16,269
5	90	166	182	194
	75	139	156	168
	50	110	127	139
	25	85	99	109
	10	61	74	83
	SD	45	44	45
	Count	16,212	13,331	15,292
6	90	177	195	204
	75	153	167	177
	50	127	140	150
	25	98	111	122
	10	68	82	93
	SD	42	45	44
	Count	10,520	9,218	11,290
7	90	180	192	202
	75	156	165	177
	50	128	136	150
	25	102	109	123
	10	79	88	98
	SD	40	43	41
	Count	6,482	4,058	5,998
8	90	185	199	199
	75	161	173	177
	50	133	146	151
	25	106	115	124
	10	77	84	97
	SD	43	45	41
	Count	5,546	3,496	5,335

potential to prevent future reading difficulties by early identification and through instructional intervention.

Assessments that measure a student's accuracy and speed in performing a skill have long been studied by researchers. Such fluency-based assessments have been proven to be efficient, reliable, and valid indicators of reading proficiency when used as screening measures (Fuchs et al., 2001; Good, Simmons, & Kame'enui, 2001). Researchers have cited a variety of studies that have documented the ability of these simple and quick measures to accurately identify individual differences in overall reading competence.

Concerns About Fluency Measures as Screening Tools

Some educators have expressed apprehension about the use of a very short measure of what may appear as a single, isolated reading skill to make a determination about a student's proficiency in the highly complex set of processes involved in the task of reading (Hamilton & Shinn, 2003). Although this concern is understandable, it is important to recognize that when fluency-based reading measures are used for screening decisions, the results are not meant to provide a full profile of a student's overall reading skill level. These measures serve as a powerful gauge of proficiency, strongly supported by a convergence of findings from decades of theoretical and empirical research (Fuchs et al., 2001; Hosp & Fuchs, 2005). The result of any screening measure must be viewed as one single piece of valuable information to be considered when making important decisions about a student, such as placement in an instructional program or possible referral for academic assistance.

ORF as a "Thermometer"

Perhaps a helpful way to explain how teachers can use a student's WCPM score as a screening tool would be to provide an analogy. A fluency-based screener can be viewed as similar to the temperature reading that a physician obtains from a thermometer when assisting a patient. A

thermometer—like a fluency-based measure—is recognized as a tool that provides valid (relevant, useful, and important) and reliable (accurate) information very quickly. However, as important as a temperature reading is to a physician, it is only a single indicator of general health or illness.

A temperature of 98.6 degrees would not result in your physician pronouncing you "well" if you have torn a ligament or have recurring headaches. On the other hand, if the thermometer reads 103 degrees, the physician is not going to rush you to surgery to have your gall bladder removed. Body temperature provides an efficient and accurate way for a doctor to gauge a patient's overall health, but it cannot fully diagnose the cause of the concern. Fluency-based screening measures can be valuable tools for teachers to use in the same way that a physician uses a thermometer—as one reasonably dependable indicator of student's academic "health" or "illness."

No assessment is perfect, and screening measures may well exemplify the type of measures sometimes referred to by education professionals as "quick and dirty." Screening measures are designed to be administered in a short period of time ("quick"), and will at times over- or underidentify students as needing assistance ("dirty"). While WCPM has been found to be a stable performance score, some variance can be expected due to several uncontrollable factors. These consist of a student's familiarity or interest in the content of the passages, a lack of precision in the timing of the passage, or mistakes made in calculating the final score due to unnoticed student errors. Both human error and measurement error are involved in every assessment. Scores from fluency-based screening measures must be considered as a performance indicator rather than a definitive cut point (Francis et al., 2005).

Using ORF Norms for Screening Decisions

Having students read for one minute in an unpracticed *grade-level* passage yields a rate and accuracy score that can be compared to the new ORF norms. This method of screening is typically used no earlier than the middle of first grade, as students' ability to read text is often not adequately developed until that time. Other fluency-based screening measures have been created for younger students who are still developing text-reading skills (Edformation, 2004; Kaminski & Good, 1998; Read Naturally, 2002). The ORF norms presented in this article start in the winter of first grade and extend up to the spring of eighth grade.

Interpreting Screening Scores Using the ORF Norms: Grade 1. Research by Good, Simmons, Kame'enui, Kaminski, & Wallin (2002) found that first-grade students who are reading 40 or more WCPM on unpracticed text passages are by the end of the year at low risk of future reading difficulty, while students below 40 WCPM are at some risk, and students reading below 20 WCPM are at high risk of failure. We recommend following these guidelines for interpreting first-grade scores.

Interpreting Screening Scores Using the ORF Norms: Grades 2-8. To determine if a student may be having difficulties with reading, the teacher compares the student's WCPM score to the scores from that student's grade level at the closest time period: fall, winter, or spring. On the basis of our field experiences with interpreting ORF screening scores, we recommend that a score falling within 10 words above or below the 50th percentile should be interpreted as within the normal, expected, and appropriate range for a student at that grade level at that time of year, at least for students in grades 2–8.

ORF Norms for Diagnosis

We can continue the medical analogy used previously with screening decisions to discuss diagnosing reading difficulties. When a physician sees a patient with an elevated body temperature, that information—along with blood pressure, cholesterol levels, height/weight ratio, and many other potential sources of data—serves as a key part of the physician's decision about the next steps to take in the patient's treatment. Diagnosing illness has direct parallels to diagnosing the causes for reading difficulties and planning appropriate instruction.

As we have discussed, if a student has a low score on a screening measure, that single score alone cannot provide the guidance we need about how to develop an instructional plan to help that student achieve academic "wellness." A professional educator looks beyond a low score on a fluency-based screening measure to examine other critical components of reading, including oral language development, phonological and phonemic awareness, phonics and decoding skills, vocabulary knowledge and language development, comprehension strategies, and reading fluency. The ORF norms can play a useful role in diagnosing possible problems that are primarily related to fluency.

Interpreting Scores Using the ORF Norms for Diagnosing Fluency Problems

The procedures for using the ORF norms to diagnose fluency problems are similar to those for screening, except here the level of materials should reflect the student's *instructional* reading level, rather than his or her *grade* level. We define instructional level as text that is challenging but manageable for the reader, with no more than approximately 1 in 10 difficult words. This translates into 90% success (Partnership for Reading, 2001).

A tool sometimes used by reading specialists or classroom teachers for diagnosing reading problems is an informal reading inventory (IRI). IRIs are either teacher-made or published sets of graded passages, sometimes with introductions to be read aloud to students before they read, and typically include a set of comprehension questions to be answered after the student reads the entire passage. IRIs are commonly used to help a teacher determine at what level a student can read text either independently or with instruction, or if the text is at that student's frustration level (less than 90% accuracy with impaired comprehension). Analysis of miscues made during the student's reading can assist in the diagnoses of decoding or comprehension difficulties. IRI passages can also be used along with CBM procedures to assist in diagnosing fluency problems.

To incorporate fluency diagnosis into an IRI assessment, a teacher would assess a student's fluency using the standardized CBM procedures during the first 60 seconds of reading in text that is determined to be at the student's *instructional* reading level.

ORF Norms for Monitoring Student Progress

A third use for ORF norms is to provide a tool to monitor a student's progress in reading. Use of CBM procedures to assess individual progress in acquiring reading skills has a long history and strong support from numerous empirical research studies (Fuchs et al., 2001; Fuchs & Fuchs, 1998; Shinn, 1989, 1998). CBM fluency-based measures have been found by many educators to be better tools for making decisions about student progress than traditional standardized measures, which can be time-consuming, expensive, administered infrequently, and of limited instructional utility (Good, Simmons, & Kame'enui, 2001; Tindal & Marston, 1990).

Using ORF Norms for Progress-Monitoring Decisions

CBM progress monitoring typically involves having a student read an unpracticed passage selected from materials at that student's grade level (for those reading at or above expected levels) or at a goal level (for students reading below expected levels). Progress-monitoring assessments may be administered weekly, once or twice monthly, or three to four times per year, depending on the type of instructional program a student is receiving.

Students at or Above Grade Level in Reading. Students whose reading performance is at or exceeds the level expected for their grade placement may need only to have their reading progress monitored a few times per year to determine if they are meeting the benchmark standards that serve as predictors of reading success. For these students, progress monitoring may take the form of simply repeating the same procedures used in the fall for screening. Students read aloud from an unpracticed passage at their grade level, and the resulting WCPM score is compared to the ORF norms for the most appropriate comparison time period—fall, winter, or spring. If a student's WCPM score is within plus or minus 10 WCPM of the 50th percentile on the ORF table, or is more than 10 WCPM above the 50th percentile, we recommend that the student be considered as making adequate progress in reading (unless there are other indicators that would raise concern).

Students Below Grade Level in Reading. For students who receive supplemental support for their reading (those reading six months to one year below grade level) or students with more serious reading problems who are getting more intensive interventions to improve their reading skills, progress monitoring may take a different form. For these students, progress-monitoring assessments may be administered more frequently, perhaps once or twice monthly for students receiving supplemental reading support, and as often as once per week for students reading more than one year below level who are receiving intensive intervention services, including special education.

Using Graphs to Interpret Progress-Monitoring Scores

When monitoring the progress of these lower performing students, the standard CBM procedures are used; however, the student's WCPM scores are recorded on a graph to facilitate interpretation of the scores. An individual progress-monitoring graph is created for each student. A graph may reflect a particular period of time, perhaps a grading period or a trimester. An aimline is placed on the graph, which represents the progress a student will need to make to achieve a preset fluency goal. Each time the student is assessed, that score is placed on the graph. If three or more consecutive scores fall below the aimline, the teacher must consider making some kind of adjustment to the current instructional program (Hasbrouck, Woldbeck, Ihnot, & Parker, 1999).

CBM progress-monitoring procedures have been available for many years but have not been widely used by teachers (Hasbrouck et al., 1999). With the increased awareness of the importance of preventing reading difficulties and providing intensive intervention as soon as a concern is noted, this will likely change. Using fluency norms to set appropriate goals for student improvement and to measure progress toward those goals is a powerful and efficient way for educators to make well-informed and timely decisions about the instructional needs of their students, particularly the lowest performing, struggling readers. (For more resources for progress monitoring, see the website of the National Center on Student Progress Monitoring at www.student progress.org.)

A Cautionary Note About Reading Fluency

We would like to add one caveat regarding reading fluency. Although this skill has recently become an increased focus in classroom reading instruction, and the awareness of the link between fluency and comprehension has grown, there appears to be a tendency among some educators to believe that raising a student's fluency score is "the" main goal of reading instruction. As important as fluency is, and as valuable as the information obtained from fluency-based assessments can be for instructional decision making, we caution teachers and administrators to keep fluency and fluency-based assessment scores in perspective. Helping our students become fluent readers is absolutely critical for proficient and motivated reading. Nonetheless, fluency is only one of the essential skills involved in reading. We suggest that teachers use the 50th percentile as a reasonable gauge of proficiency for students. Keep in mind that it is appropriate and expected

for students to adjust their rate when reading text of varying difficulty and for varied purposes. Pushing every student to reach the 90th percentile or even the 75th percentile in their grade level is not a reasonable or appropriate goal for fluency instruction.

Focus on Fluency

Reading is a complex process involving multiple linguistic and cognitive challenges. It is clear that the ability to read text effortlessly, quickly, accurately, and with expression plays an essential role in becoming a competent reader. Researchers still have much work to do to identify fully the features, mechanisms, and processes involved in reading fluency. However, decades of research have validated the use of fluency-based measures for making essential decisions about which students may need assistance in becoming a skilled reader (screening), an individual student's strength or need with the skills of reading fluency (diagnosis), and whether a student is making adequate progress toward the goals of improved reading proficiency (progress monitoring). While we strongly agree with the premise that accuracy, rate, and quality of oral reading must be assessed within a context of comprehension (Pikulski & Chard, 2005), up-to-date national oral reading fluency norms can serve as an important tool to assist educators in developing, implementing, and evaluating effective instructional programs to help every student become a skilled, lifelong reader and learner.

References

Adams, G.N., & Brown, S. (2003). *The six-minute solution*. Longmont, CO: Sopris West.

Behavioral Research and Teaching. (2005). *Oral reading fluency: 90 years of assessment* (Tech. Rep. No. 33). Eugene: University of Oregon.

Cassidy, J., & Cassidy, D. (December 2004/January 2005). What's hot, what's not for 2005. *Reading Today*, p. 1.

Edformation. (2004). *AIMSweb progress monitoring and assessment system*. Retrieved May 17, 2004, from http://www.edformation.com

Francis, D.J., Fletcher, J.M., Stuebing, K.K., Lyon, G.R., Shaywitz, B.A., & Shaywitz, S.E. (2005). Psychometric approaches to the identification of LD: IQ and achievement scores are not sufficient. *Journal of Intellectual Disabilities, 38*(2), 98–108.

Fuchs, L.S., & Deno, S.L. (1991). Curriculum-based measurement: Current applications and future directions. *Exceptional Children, 57,* 466–501.

Fuchs, L.S., & Fuchs, D. (1998). Monitoring student progress toward the development of reading competence: A review of three forms of classroom-based assessment. *School Psychology Review, 28,* 659–671.

Fuchs, L.S., Fuchs, D., Hosp, M.K., & Jenkins, J.R. (2001). Oral reading fluency as an indicator of reading competence: A theoretical, empirical, and historical analysis. *Scientific Studies of Reading, 5,* 239–256.

Good, R.H., III, & Kaminski, R.A. (Eds.). (2002). *Dynamic indicators of basic early literacy skills* (6th ed.). Eugene: University of Oregon, Institute for the Development of Educational Achievement.

Good, R.H., Simmons, D.C., & Kame'enui, E.J. (2001). The importance and decision-making utility of a continuum of fluency-based indicators of foundational reading skills for third-grade high-stakes outcomes. *Scientific Studies of Reading, 5,* 257–288.

Good, R.H., Simmons, D.S., Kame'enui, E.J., Kaminski, R.A., & Wallin, J. (2002). *Summary of decision rules for intensive, strategic, and benchmark instructional recommendations in kindergarten through third grade* (Tech. Rep. No. 11). Eugene: University of Oregon.

Hamilton, C., & Shinn, M.R. (2003). Characteristics of word callers: An investigation of the accuracy of teachers' judgments of reading comprehension and oral reading skills. *School Psychology Review, 32,* 228–240.

Hasbrouck, J.E., & Tindal, G. (1992). Curriculum-based oral reading fluency norms for students in grades 2–5. *Teaching Exceptional Children, 24*(3), 41–44.

Hasbrouck, J.E., Woldbeck, T., Ihnot, C., & Parker, R.I. (1999). One teacher's use of curriculum-based measurement: A changed opinion. *Learning Disabilities Research & Practice, 14*(2), 118–126.

Hiebert, E.H. (2002). *QuickReads.* Upper Saddle River, NJ: Modern Curriculum Press.

Hosp, M.K., & Fuchs, L.S. (2005). Using CBM as an indicator of decoding, word reading, and comprehension: Do the relations change with grade? *School Psychology Review, 34,* 9–26.

Hudson, R.F., Lane, H.B., & Pullen, P.C. (2005). Reading fluency assessment and instruction: What, why, and how? *The Reading Teacher, 58,* 702–714.

Ihnot, C. (1991). *Read naturally.* Minneapolis, MN: Read Naturally.

Kame'enui, E.J. (2002, May). *Final report on the analysis of reading assessment instruments for K–3.* Eugene:

University of Oregon, Institute for the Development of Educational Achievement.

Kaminski, R.A., & Good, R.H. (1998). Assessing early literacy skills in a problem-solving model: Dynamic Indicators of Basic Early Literacy Skills. In M.R. Shinn (Ed.), *Advanced applications of curriculum-based measurement* (pp. 113–142). New York: Guilford.

Kuhn, M. (2004/2005). Helping students become accurate, expressive readers: Fluency instruction for small groups. *The Reading Teacher, 58,* 338–345.

Linn, R.L. (2000). Assessments and accountability. *Educational Researcher, 29*(2), 4–16.

McLaughlin, M.J., & Thurlow, M. (2003). Educational accountability and students with disabilities: Issues and challenges. *Educational Policy, 17,* 431–451.

National Institute of Child Health and Human Development. (2000). *Report of the National Reading Panel. Teaching children to read: An evidence-based assessment of the scientific research literature on reading and its implications for reading instruction* (NIH Publication No. 00–4769). Washington, DC: U.S. Government Printing Office.

No Child Left Behind Act of 2001, Pub. L. No. 107–110, 115 Stat. 1425 (2002).

Osborn, J., & Lehr, F. (2004). *A focus on fluency.* Honolulu, HI: Pacific Resources for Education and Learning.

Partnership for Reading. (2001). *Put reading first: The research building blocks for teaching children to read.* Washington, DC: National Institute for Literacy.

Pikulski, J.J., & Chard, D.J. (2005). Fluency: Bridge between decoding and comprehension. *The Reading Teacher, 58,* 510–519.

Rasinski, T.V. (2004). *Assessing reading fluency.* Honolulu, HI: Pacific Resources for Education and Learning.

Read Naturally. (2002). *Reading fluency monitor.* Minneapolis: Author.

Shinn, M.R. (Ed.). (1989). *Curriculum-based measurement: Assessing special children.* New York: Guilford.

Shinn, M.R. (Ed.). (1998). *Advanced applications of curriculum-based measurement.* New York: Guilford.

Snow, C.E., Burns, M.S., & Griffin, P. (Eds.). (1998). *Preventing reading difficulties in young children.* Washington, DC: National Academy Press.

Stahl, S.A., & Kuhn, M.R. (2002). Making it sound like language: Developing fluency. *The Reading Teacher, 55,* 582–584.

Texas Education Agency. (2004). *Texas primary reading inventory—TPRI.* Retrieved May 19, 2005, from http://www.tpri.org

Tindal, G., & Marston, D. (1990). *Classroom-based assessment: Testing for teachers.* Columbus, OH: Merrill.

Questions for Reflection

• How do your students compare on the oral reading fluency norms provided in this article? What does this tell you about their automaticity in reading? Do you see any correlation between their oral reading fluency scores (words correct per minute) and their achievement on other indicators of reading success?

• The authors note that "Some educators have expressed apprehension about the use of a very short measure of what may appear as a single, isolated reading skill to make a determination about a student's proficiency in the highly complex set of processes involved in the task of reading." They also explain that these measures are not intended to provide a full picture of a student's proficiency. How are measures of students' oral reading rate used in your school or district? How can you ensure that they are used appropriately to support students?

Speed Does Matter in Reading

Timothy V. Rasinski

As a director of a university diagnostic reading clinic, I see children of all ages who, for one reason or another, are making poor progress in learning to read. Our job in the reading clinic is to determine the nature and source of the child's reading problem and suggest (and implement) instructional interventions for helping the child improve. Often the children we see in our clinic demonstrate remarkable strengths. Many have excellent vocabularies; they know the meanings of many words. Others manage to read with few errors in word recognition. Still others often demonstrate high levels of comprehension, even when their oral reading of a passage is marked by a large number of uncorrected word recognition errors. One of the most common manifestations of reading problems in the children we see, however, is slow, disfluent, or what we have come to call inefficient reading. Even when these children have adequate comprehension of a passage, their reading is often characterized by slow, labored, inexpressive, and unenthusiastic rendering of a passage.

Wondering if this manifestation of slow reading among struggling readers is present in readers other than those seen in our reading clinic, my colleague Nancy Padak and I examined all the children in Grades 2 through 5 referred for Title I reading services by their teachers in the Akron, Ohio public schools—over 600 students (Rasinski & Padak, 1998). We asked these children to read a passage at their assigned grade level and one below their grade placement using standard informal reading inventory procedures. What we found surprised us.

The informal reading inventory criteria showed that students' comprehension and word recognition were, on average, at their frustration level—but they were near the threshold for instructional-level reading. In other words, comprehension and word recognition were poor, but it wouldn't take much improvement to move their performance to an instructional level. Reading rate, however, was a different story. When reading passages at their grade level, these students, who their teachers identified as struggling readers, read at a rate that was approximately 60% of their instructional level reading rate; for a passage below their grade level the rate was 50% (Rasinski, 1999). Clearly reading rate, or speed, was a significant factor in classroom teachers' perceptions of their students' proficiency or lack of proficiency in reading.

Excessively Slow, Disfluent Reading Leads to Less Overall Reading

It is interesting and, to me, somewhat ironic that slow and labored reading rate may be a reason teachers see fit to recommend certain of their students for supplementary reading services such as Title I. Often when I speak with teachers about reading fluency I mention that reading rate may be an indicator of fluent or disfluent reading. This frequently results in concern expressed by some in the audience that reading rate or reading speed should not be considered a significant factor in reading. This concern is often expressed in a comment like this: "As long as students understand what they read, as long as they are making meaning out of the text, reading rate should not matter." While I certainly and absolutely agree that understanding what is read is the end game for reading, reading rate, or

Reprinted from Rasinski, T.V. (2000). Speed does matter in reading. *The Reading Teacher, 54*(2), 146–151.

speed, cannot be ignored either as an indicator of reading fluency or, more precisely, as evidence of excessively slow processing of text. The simple fact that slow reading requires readers to invest considerably greater amounts of time in the reading task than classmates who are reading at a rate appropriate for their grade level should be a major cause for concern for all teachers.

Most of us would agree that reading progress is determined to a large extent by the amount of reading one does (Anderson, Wilson, & Fielding, 1988; Postlethwaite & Ross, 1992). Slow readers, however, by definition, read fewer words per given amount of time than readers who read at more normal rates. Thus, just to keep up with their classmates in the amount of reading done, these slower readers have to invest considerably more time and energy in their reading.

Indeed, data from the 1992 National Assessment of Educational Progress (NAEP) (Pinnell et al., 1995) demonstrate a relationship between reading rate and fluency and self-selected reading in and out of school. The most fluent readers tended to be self-motivated, while less fluent readers were less likely to read in class or out of school. While the causal nature of this relationship has not been empirically established, it seems reasonable to assume that fluency in reading leads to greater reading and greater reading leads to gains in fluency—fluency and reading volume are cause and consequence of one another. (See Stanovich, 1985, for a more complete description of this phenomenon he termed the Matthew effect.)

Excessively Slow, Disfluent Reading Is Associated With Poor Comprehension

Moreover, for most children, slow reading is associated with poor comprehension and poor overall reading performance. Research dating back over 60 years suggests that faster readers tend to have better comprehension over what is read and tend to be, overall, more proficient readers (Carver, 1990, Pinnell et al., 1995). The 1992 NAEP study found that 15% of all fourth

graders (one out of seven) read "no faster than 74 words per minute...a pace at which it would be difficult to keep track of ideas as they are developing within the sentence and across the page" (Pinnell et al., 1995, p. 42). Indeed, the same 1992 NAEP study found that holistic ratings of reading fluency as well as fourth graders' reading rates were associated with overall reading proficiency (Pinnell et al., 1995; White, 1995). Slow, disfluent reading, then, is linked with poor comprehension. This leads to students reading less, which in turn results in their making slower progress in reading than students who read at a more normal rate for their age or grade placement.

Excessively Slow Reading Leads to Reading Frustration

Even at the classroom instruction level, slow reading has negative consequences. Imagine yourself as a fifth-grade student who is assigned to read a 12-page chapter in a social studies book in school. Imagine also that you are a disfluent or inefficient reader. You read at 58 words per minute (the average reading rate when reading grade level material of fifth graders referred for Title I support, Rasinski & Padak, 1998), or about half the rate of your classmates. You begin reading as best you can. Like most students, you are well aware of what is happening around you. You are about halfway through the passage, and you notice that many of your classmates have finished reading—they are done and you still have six pages to read. What do you do? Do you pretend to have completed the assignment even though you haven't read or comprehended the entire passage? Or, do you continue reading knowing that by doing so you will be broadcasting your lack of reading proficiency and making your classmates wait on you? Neither solution is very palatable, yet the problem is all too common.

Even if an assignment were made for home reading, the 60-minute reading assignment for most students would become 2 hours of reading for you. Checking out of the reading club may be just around the corner. You may become a

9-year-old (one out of eight as reported by the NAEP) who claims never or hardly ever to read for fun. And if you don't read, chances are your progress in reading will continue to decelerate. Clearly, excessively slow and disfluent reading is an indicator of concern.

Helping Slow Readers

How do we help slow readers? Does slow inefficient reading require putting students into some sort of special regimen or treatment for increasing reading rate? Absolutely not. For most readers, a slow reading rate, one that lacks flow or fluency, suggests that the student is an inefficient reader. Although the student may have some success in decoding words, it is far from a smooth, automatic, and efficient process—the kind that requires little investment of attention or cognitive energy. The slow reader has to devote so much time and attention to decoding that overall reading pace is significantly reduced; moreover, cognitive resources that could have been used for comprehension must be reallocated to word recognition (LaBerge & Samuels, 1974). As a result, comprehension suffers. Slow, disfluent reading may also be associated with a lack of sensitivity to meaningful phrasing and syntax (how words are ordered and organized in sentences within a passage) that also helps the reader construct the meaning of text (Schreiber, 1980).

Improving students' word recognition efficiency and helping readers develop greater sensitivity to the syntactic nature of the text will result in more efficient reading and improved reading rate or fluency. But again, this does not have to be achieved through isolated skills practice or boring drills. Reading rate, efficiency, or fluency can be developed through instructional activities such as repeated readings, especially authentic ways, such as practicing poetry or scripts for later performance, and supported reading when it is done in activities where the reader reads an authentic text but is supported by a more fluent partner.

One key to nurturing fluent reading is finding the appropriate text for the reader to read.

Texts that are too difficult, overly dense with unfamiliar vocabulary and concepts, can make any otherwise fluent reader disfluent (if you don't believe this, try reading aloud an unfamiliar legal document or a selection from a textbook on nuclear physics). Thus, it is important that we find texts that are well within the reader's independent-instructional range in order to promote fluency. Short, highly predictable selections that are meant to be read aloud and with expression, such as rhyming poetry, are ideal for reading fluency instruction.

Poetry and reading fluency are an excellent match in nearly any classroom and for all students. Integrating poetry into the reading curriculum is a great way to promote fluent reading through repeated reading of readable and intriguing texts. However, despite the wonderful potential of poetry to explore language, it is one of the most often neglected components of the language arts curriculum (Denman, 1988; Perfect, 1999). Turning poetry into a performance, which it is meant to be (Graves, 1992; Perfect, 1999), and turning away from too much critical analysis, can give poetry its rightful place in the reading-language arts curriculum. Moreover, when poetry performance is fostered in the classroom, reading fluency is also nurtured as students attempt to make their oral interpretations just right—and this means repeated readings, but in a very natural and purposeful way.

In some classrooms I have visited, teachers simply select a day for a poetry party. Several days prior to the event, students select a poem to learn from one of the poetry books and anthologies in the teacher's personal collection or from a library, or they compose their own poem. Over the next several days students practice reading their poems, usually from a variety of perspectives, in preparation for the poetry party.

When the poetry party day finally arrives, the overhead lights in the classroom are dimmed, a lamp on the teacher's desk is turned on, hot apple cider and popcorn are served, and students take turns performing their poems for their classmates and other visitors. Students' expressive and interpretive readings of their poems are responded to with warm applause (or, harkening back to a previous generation, with the snapping of fingers). I'll never forget the cold, snowy day in January when a fourth grader gave a heartfelt rendition of *The Cremation of Sam McGee* (Service, 1907/1986). I can still feel the shivers it sent down my spine.

Readers Theatre is another very natural and authentic way to promote repeated readings. Readers Theatre does not rely on costumes, movement, props, or scenery to express meaning—just the performers and their voices as they face their audience with script in hand. For students to perform a Readers Theatre script in a meaningful and engaging manner, they need to practice the script beforehand. Students love to perform for an audience when they are given sufficient opportunities to rehearse the script. In a 10-week implementation of Readers Theatre in which small groups of second-grade students were introduced to, practiced, and performed a new script each week, students made significant gains in reading rate and overall reading achievement as measured by an informal reading inventory (Martinez, Roser, & Strecker, 1999). Through the repeated readings inherent in preparation for Readers Theatre, students made an average rate gain of 17 words per minute, about the gain that could be expected in an entire year (Rasinski, 1999), while students engaged in more traditional reading activities made less than half the gain the Readers Theatre students experienced. In addition to its application in classroom settings, Rinehart (1999) found that Readers Theatre was a particularly effective and motivating approach for students experiencing reading difficulties.

Paired reading (Topping, 1987), echo reading, choral reading, and reading with talking books are ways to provide support for less fluent readers. Topping (1987), for example, found that paired reading could significantly accelerate students' reading fluency and overall proficiency. In our university reading clinic we ask parents of struggling readers to engage in a form of paired reading with their children for 10 to 15 minutes each evening. In our version of paired reading, parents read a brief poem or passage to their children. This is followed by the parent and child

reading the text together several times. Finally, the child reads the text to the parent; the parent responds to the child's reading with enthusiastic and authentic praise for a job well done. We have found that children who engage in this form of paired reading make significant gains (in as little as 5 weeks) over children who receive clinical tutoring without the parental paired reading support (Rasinski, 1995). Similar types of paired and supported reading done in the classroom with less fluent readers have been found to result in improvements in reading rate and overall reading achievement (Rasinski, Padak, Linek, & Sturtevant, 1994).

Buddy reading is another excellent example of how teachers can create complex instructional scenarios that are engaging, authentic, and lead to gains in fluency. Let's look at a third grader who is having trouble reading. We know that repeated readings lead to fluency gains (Samuels, 1979). We also know that supported reading in the form of paired reading will also lead to gains in fluency, word recognition, and comprehension (Topping, 1987). This child's third-grade teacher, cognizant of his struggle with fluency, decides, with the child's permission, to pair this third grader with a second grader who is also having difficulty in reading. The third grader will meet with the second grader twice a week and read with her a passage from one of the second grader's textbooks for about 20 minutes. In anticipation of each meeting, the third grader needs to practice the assigned passage (which will be somewhat easier for the third grader to read because it is at a difficulty level appropriate for the second grader) so that he can read it with accuracy and expression with his partner. This may require two or three or more readings of the passage. Yet the third grader does so enthusiastically, for he has a real reason to practice.

When the partners read, first the third grader reads the passage to his partner, then they read it together once or twice, and then, if time allows, the second grader reads it while the partner follows along and provides support and encouragement. The practice is natural and the outcome is clear. Through repeated readings of somewhat easier texts the third grader makes significant strides in his reading fluency and overall reading. The second grader, with the additional modeled and paired reading support, makes significant gains in her reading as well.

The opportunities to create authentic and engaging reading instruction that meets the needs of all readers, but especially inefficient and disfluent readers, are enormous. Creative and informed teachers have been designing reading instruction that meets the needs of their students for years. We need to empower all teachers to do the same. Teachers need to be aware of children's needs and plan accordingly with instruction that meets those needs. Slow, disfluent reading is one indication of a problem for a significant number of young readers.

The goal in fluency instruction is not fast reading, although that often happens to be a byproduct of the instruction, but fluent and meaning-filled reading. To this end I have found that reading to students is a wonderful way to model the connection between fluent reading and meaningful reading. Often I will read to students in as meaningful and expressive a voice as possible. Then, after I have read the selection and discussed its meaning with students, I will draw their attention to my reading of the passage. I will ask them to remember how I read the passage and how my expressiveness affected their understanding. "What did that long pause in my reading make you think? What happened when I read this part in a soft voice? How did my reading this section fast and loud affect how you understood this part of the story? And when I read these words very slow and deliberately, what did that do for for you?" Sometimes I will read a poem or text from various points of view: as if I am angry, as if I am calm, or as if I am nervous. Then I will discuss with students how the expression I embedded in the words helped to communicate to the listener my own point of view. This sort of reading and discussion helps students develop a metacognitive understanding that the meaning of a passage is not carried only in the words, but also in the way the words are presented to the reader. It also provides a model for students' own meaningful, expressive, and contextualized reading, whether orally to an audience or silently with that inner voice that is heard only by the reader.

Reading to students and discussing the nature of the reading allows us to focus on the flexible attitude readers need to bring to the reading act. Fluent and understandable reading, not fast reading, is the goal of our instruction. Fluent reading is often quick paced, but not always. Sometimes, especially with difficult, technical, expository, or unfamiliar content texts, readers need to slow down and process texts more deliberately. Reading these more challenging passages to students and discussing their understanding helps students realize that a truly fluent reader is one who is able to adjust his or her reading rate according to the challenge posed by the text and the information the reader needs to get from the text.

Do Not Ignore Reading Rate

I do not wish to take anything away from comprehension as the desired and ultimate result of reading and reading instruction. Rather, the point I am hoping to make is that we need to take the notion of slow, inefficient, disfluent reading seriously. Even with adequate comprehension, slow and labored reading will turn any school or recreational reading assignment into a marathon of frustration for nearly any student.

A slow reading rate may be symptomatic of inefficient word recognition or lack of sensitivity to the phrase—the natural unit of meaning in reading. But these problems can be addressed through authentic and engaging instructional activities and routines that can be woven seamlessly into the regular reading curriculum and that are appropriate for all students, not just those identified as disfluent. As reading teachers, diagnosticians, and specialists, we need to be aware of the importance of reading rate as a diagnostic indicator and to use reading rate as one of many tools for assessing students' overall reading performance. To ignore reading rate when assessing children's reading and designing appropriate instruction may do a major disservice to many readers who struggle with reading.

References

Anderson, R.C., Wilson, P.T., & Fielding, L.G. (1988). Growth in reading and how children spend their time outside of school. *Reading Research Quarterly, 23,* 285–303.

Carver, R.P. (1990). *Reading rate: A review of research and theory.* San Diego, CA: Academic Press.

Denman, G.A. (1988). *When you've made it your own...: Teaching poetry to young people.* Portsmouth, NH: Heinemann.

Graves, D.H. (1992). *The reading/writing teacher's companion: Explore poetry.* Portsmouth, NH: Heinemann.

LaBerge, D., & Samuels, S.J. (1974). Toward a theory of automatic information processing in reading. *Cognitive Psychology, 6,* 293–323.

Martinez, M., Roser, N., & Strecker, S. (1999). "I never thought I could be a star": A Readers Theatre ticket to fluency. *The Reading Teacher, 52,* 326–334.

Perfect, K.A. (1999). Rhyme and reason: Poetry for the heart and head. *The Reading Teacher, 52,* 728–737.

Pinnell, G.S., Pikulski, J.J., Wixson, K.K., Campbell, J.R., Gough, P.B., & Beatty, A.S. (1995). *Listening to children read aloud.* Washington, DC: U.S. Department of Education, National Center for Education Statistics.

Postlethwaite, T.N., & Ross, K.N. (1992). *Effective schools in reading.* The Hague: International Association for the Evaluation of Educational Achievement.

Rasinski, T.V. (1995). Fast Start: A parent involvement reading program for primary grade students. In W. Linek & E. Sturtevant (Eds.), *Generations of literacy: The 17th yearbook of the College Reading Association* (pp. 301–312). Harrisonburg, VA: College Reading Association.

Rasinski, T.V. (1999). Exploring a method for estimating independent, instructional, and frustration reading rates. *Reading Psychology: An International Quarterly, 20,* 61–69.

Rasinski, T.V., & Padak, N. (1998). How elementary students referred for compensatory reading instruction perform on school-based measures of word recognition, fluency, and comprehension. *Reading Psychology: An International Quarterly, 19,* 185–216.

Rasinski, T.V., Padak, N., Linek, W.L., & Sturtevant, E. (1994). Effects of fluency development on urban second-grade readers. *Journal of Educational Research, 87,* 158–165.

Rinehart, S. (1999). "Don't think for a minute that I'm getting up there": Opportunities for readers' theater in a tutorial for children with reading problems. *Reading Psychology: An International Quarterly, 20,* 71–89.

Samuels, S.J. (1979). The method of repeated readings. *The Reading Teacher, 32,* 403–408.

Schreiber, P.A. (1980). On the acquisition of reading fluency. *Journal of Reading Behavior, 12,* 177–186.

Service, R. (1986). *The cremation of Sam McGee.* New York: Greenwillow. (Original work published 1907)

Stanovich, K.E. (1985). Matthew effects in reading: Some consequences of individual differences in the acquisition of literacy. *Reading Research Quarterly, 21,* 360–407.

Topping, K. (1987). Paired Reading: A powerful technique for parent use. *The Reading Teacher, 40,* 608–614.

White, S. (1995). *Listening to children read aloud: Oral fluency.* Washington, DC: U.S. Office of Education, Office of Educational Research and Improvement.

Questions for Reflection

• As the author describes, struggling readers often get caught in a cycle: They need practice in order to improve their reading achievement, but because they read disfluently, the amount they read and their confidence in reading are low—and so they do not get the practice they need to improve. Do you have sufficient texts at a variety of reading instructional levels to ensure that *all* learners in your classroom have access to reading materials that will allow them to experience success? If you work with older learners, how do you ensure that texts match both the reading levels and the increasingly sophisticated and mature interests of your students?

• Reading rate is one measure of a student's overall reading achievement. What measures do you use in addition to reading rate? In what ways do you use data from all these measures to form a complete picture of a student's reading and to inform your instruction? Do you have any concerns with using reading rate as a measure?

Reading Fluency Instruction: Moving Beyond Accuracy, Automaticity, and Prosody

Timothy V. Rasinski

The longer I live, the more I see there's something about reciting rhythmical words aloud—it's almost biological—that comforts and enlivens human beings.

Robert Pinsky, 1997–2000 Poet Laureate of the United States

This is my first column for the Issues and Trends in Literacy department [in the journal *The Reading Teacher*, where this article was originally published] after taking over from the previous editor, Linda Gambrell. In it I write on a topic about which I feel most knowledgeable—reading fluency. Moreover, because reading fluency is increasingly recognized as critical to students' literacy development, it is important to continue a professional conversation and dialogue on the topic. To this end, then, I use an article from the May 2005 issue of *The Reading Teacher* as the starting point for my commentary on this emerging and important issue in reading education.

In the May 2005 article "Reading fluency assessment and instruction: What, why, and how?" Roxanne Hudson, Holly Lane, and Paige Pullen did a masterful job of defining and describing three key elements of reading fluency: accuracy in word decoding, automaticity in recognizing words, and appropriate use of prosody or meaningful oral expression while reading. These three components are a gateway to comprehension. Readers must be able to decode words correctly and effortlessly (automaticity) and then put them together into meaningful phrases with the appropriate expression to make sense of what they read.

Too many developing readers (a) make an excessive number of decoding errors while reading; (b) read words in text correctly but put such effort into the task that they exhaust their cognitive resources, which should be devoted to comprehension; or (c) decode words accurately and effortlessly but are unable to put them together in a way that adds appropriate and meaningful expression to their oral reading. The result of any of these manifestations is often poor comprehension, a decided lack of enthusiasm for reading, and a personal sense of failure.

In addition to defining reading fluency, Hudson et al. gave some solid suggestions for teaching each area of fluency. Although their recommendations are valid and based in the research literature, I am a bit concerned for several reasons. Implied in their presentation of fluency instruction methods is the notion that word accuracy and automaticity should be taught separately from prosodic reading. Accuracy and automaticity, they suggested, are best taught through methods aimed at improving student reading rate—the way to measure progress in these areas. Prosody in reading is taught through modeling, performance, focus on phrasing, assisted reading techniques, and explicit instruction on appropriate intonation.

Reprinted from Rasinski, T. (2006). Reading fluency instruction: Moving beyond accuracy, automaticity, and prosody. *The Reading Teacher*, 59(7), 704–706.

I have no quarrel with the methods they present for teaching fluency, but I do have two concerns about the notion of teaching the components of fluency separately. First, dividing this instruction requires extra time to teach each component: Time must be given to accuracy and automaticity, and additional time must be given to prosody. We all know that time is precious in any instructional setting, and having to provide separate instruction in each of these areas is not efficient. My second concern about the segmentation described is the message it sends to students (and teachers) about the goal of fluency instruction, particularly with the repeated reading instruction aimed at improving word-recognition automaticity. Because improvements in automaticity are determined by gains in reading rate, it is not difficult to see why students (and teachers) begin to focus almost exclusively on improving reading rate as the goal for fluency instruction. Indeed, the primary aim of many instructional programs is to increase reading rate through repeated reading of nonfiction material. It is not unreasonable, then, to suspect that students in such programs would perseverate on reading faster for the sake of reading faster, without giving commensurate attention to comprehension. The result of such a focus is faster reading with little improvement on comprehension, which is the ultimate goal of reading and reading instruction.

There are dedicated and well-meaning teachers who have taken this goal of improving reading rate to heart and focused their instruction on improving students' reading rate through repeated readings and other rate-building activities. Students in these classrooms have become faster readers, but their reading comprehension has not improved. Students learn what we teach them. Indeed, a new generation of students is appearing at U.S. university reading clinics, students who have learned to read fast but are poor comprehenders and poor readers.

I fear that a single-minded focus on using repeated reading to improve reading rate, without commensurate emphasis on reading for meaning, will not have the desired result of improving comprehension and will eventually re-turn reading fluency to a secondary role in the curriculum.

Good Fluency Instruction

I think that instruction on accuracy, automaticity, and prosodic reading can and should occur in unison—in an integrated and synergistic manner. Here is how I see good fluency instruction. First, I do agree with Hudson et al. that repeated reading is one of the best ways to develop fluency. But then I ask myself, what would make me or anyone else want to engage in repeated reading? To improve my rate of reading? Not really. What would really inspire me to engage in repeated reading or rehearsal is performance. If I were to give an oral reading performance of a passage, I would most certainly have an incentive to practice, rehearse, or engage in repeated readings. All of us, at one time or another, have read orally for an audience. It is likely that we practiced in advance of that reading, and if we didn't it is likely that we wish we had.

To continue with this line of reasoning, if performance is the incentive to practice, then we need to ask what kinds of texts lend themselves to expressive oral performance? Informational texts? Not likely. Despite other important qualities, they do not lend themselves easily to expressive interpretation. Narrative material? Perhaps. However, there are several other text genres that are specifically meant to be performed or that are easy to perform—rhythmical, rhetorical, or interactive texts such as poetry, song lyrics, chants, rhymes, plays (Readers Theatre), monologues, dialogues, and letters. Such texts work well for oral reading with expression and meaning, not just speed. To me these texts are the perfect fit for fluency instruction and repeated readings. Moreover, these legitimate genres have largely been left out of the U.S. school reading curriculum. By using them, teachers expose students to a wider variety of reading genres, and by practicing and performing them, students gain in accuracy, automaticity (rate), prosody, *and* comprehension.

Classroom research has shown that this approach to repeated readings has helped students make remarkable progress in reading rate (even though improving reading rate was not emphasized). General growth in reading and, perhaps most significant, enjoyment of reading have also increased. In their study of second graders' use of Readers Theatre, Martinez, Roser, and Strecker (1999) found that students doing repeated readings with Readers Theatre made twice the gain in reading rate than a comparison group, even though the focus of the repeated reading was on expressive, meaning-filled reading and not on speed. The Readers Theatre students also made substantially greater progress than the comparison group on an informal reading inventory—a measure of reading that includes reading comprehension as well as fluency. Moreover, students doing Readers Theatre loved to practice because they would later perform the materials they had rehearsed for an audience. Second grader Lucia wrote in her journal, "I never thought I could be a star, but I was the best reader today" (p. 333).

In another second-grade study of repeated readings (Rasinski, Padak, Linek, & Sturtevant, 1994), struggling readers who rehearsed and then performed poetry and other performance texts made significantly greater gains in reading rate than students reading but not rehearsing and performing the same material.

In a study of first graders rehearsing poetry with their parents each night (Rasinski & Stevenson, 2005), students most at risk for failure in reading made nearly two-and-a-half times the progress in reading rate as students who read the poetry with their parents but did not rehearse it. As in the previous studies, the emphasis was on reading with expression, enthusiasm, and meaning, not speed. Nevertheless, reading speed (as well as other indicators of reading proficiency) showed significant improvement.

Similar results have been seen with older students. Working in her own fourth-grade classroom, Lorraine Griffith (Griffith & Rasinski, 2004) found that a weekly program of practicing and then performing Readers Theatre scripts and poetry resulted in a reading rate gain of 48.2 words correct per minute for her Title I students. (Title I is a U.S. federally funded program for at-risk students.) This represents an improvement

that is more than double the approximately 15–20 word-count-per-minute gain that is expected of normally developing fourth graders (Hudson et al., 2005). Yet, throughout Griffith's work with students, the emphasis was on repeated reading for expression and meaning, not speed. Although she later incorporated a timed reading segment into her fluency program, she chose texts of high literary quality that could easily be performed, and she kept the focus on reading with meaningful expression.

Repeated Reading Is Key

My purpose in this column is to reinforce the recommendation by Hudson et al. that repeated reading is a key instructional method for developing reading fluency. I also wish to express a strong concern that the aim of repeated reading should be meaningful and expressive oral interpretation or performance of text, not faster reading. To that end, certain texts lend themselves to oral interpretive reading. Those are the ones teachers should be looking for and using in fluency instruction. Indeed, if such texts become the focus and content of reading fluency instruction then students will also know the sense of comfort and vitality that poet Robert Pinsky says comes from reading rhythmical words aloud.

References

Hudson, R.F., Lane, H.B., & Pullen, P.C. (2005). Reading fluency assessment and instruction: What, why, and how? *The Reading Teacher, 58*, 702–714.

Griffith, L.W., & Rasinski, T.V. (2004). A focus on fluency: How one teacher incorporated fluency with her reading curriculum. *The Reading Teacher, 58*, 126–137.

Martinez, M., Roser, N., & Strecker, S. (1999). "I never thought I could be a star": A Readers Theatre ticket to reading fluency. *The Reading Teacher, 52*, 326–334.

Rasinski, T.V., Padak, N.D., Linek, W.L., & Sturtevant, E. (1994). Effects of fluency development on urban second-grade readers. *Journal of Educational Research, 87*, 158–165.

Rasinski, T.V., & Stevenson, B. (2005). The effects of Fast Start Reading: A fluency-based home involvement reading program, on the reading achievement of beginning readers. *Reading Psychology: An International Journal, 26*, 109–125.

Question for Reflection

• Consider this article in its position as the final piece in this collection. After having read these articles, how do you now conceptualize fluency as a component of the reading curriculum? How does it "fit" between or beside decoding and comprehension? How will you modify your instruction to contribute both to students' growth in fluency and to their overall growth in reading?